Grade 2

Credits
Author: Angela Triplett
Copy Editor: Carrie Fox

Visit *carsondellosa.com* for correlations to Common Core, state, national, and Canadian provincial standards.

Carson-Dellosa Publishing LLC
PO Box 35665
Greensboro, NC 27425 USA
carsondellosa.com

ISBN 978-1-4838-3845-8
02-257187784

Table of Contents

What Is Math Workshop?

One of the most challenging aspects of teaching mathematics is differentiating instruction to meet the needs of all of the learners in your classroom. As a classroom teacher, you are responsible for teaching the standards that must be met by the end of the year. But, the reality inside the classroom is that one size does not fit all. For some students, the material is too difficult. For others, it is too easy.

With both reading and writing, many teachers have found the workshop model to be an excellent way to teach students at various levels. It allows for whole-group and small-group instruction, and individual practice so teachers can monitor students' progress and vary instruction according to need. The same workshop approach can be used for successful math instruction. This model encourages students to go beyond passive learning and become mathematicians who can think critically.

Like reading and writing workshops, math workshop is a structure, not a curriculum. It can be used with existing curriculums and materials and should be adapted to best fit the needs of the teacher and students. Math workshop will look different from classroom to classroom but usually includes the same building blocks: a warm-up, a whole-class mini-lesson, leveled small-group instruction, and individual practice. For a more in-depth look at the elements of math workshop, refer to pages 4 and 5.

Using a math workshop model allows teachers to:
- meet the needs of learners at all levels
- encourage deeper learning than in traditional lessons
- spiral concepts throughout the year
- work with any curriculum
- group students flexibly so they can move according to their changing needs
- offer repeated opportunities for practice
- keep students consistently engaged in learning

Starting math workshop in your classroom can seem overwhelming if you've never done it before. Use the guides on pages 4 through 14 to help you decide how math workshop will work in your classroom, plan your lessons, and manage the day-to-day details. Then, get started with over 25 preplanned lessons and activities. Use the blank reproducible activities starting on page 183 to create your own practice and review activities to be used throughout the year.

The Elements of Math Workshop

The major parts of math workshop are a warm-up, a mini-lesson, rotations (which include guided math groups, independent practice, and conferencing), and closure. You do not have to follow this format exactly. Instead, mix, match, and tweak things to make math workshop work for your classroom. See page 6 for more information on how math workshop can be changed to better fit your needs. Once you understand the basics, you can use the information below to plan your own math workshop lessons. Refer to pages 9 and 10 for more information on planning math workshop lessons.

1 Warm-Up
about 5 minutes

The warm-up is used to get students thinking mathematically and prepare them for the mini-lesson. It can be the same every day, or changed to relate to the lesson focus. You may choose to discuss only a portion of the assignment, such as a few sections of the calendar bulletin board or a single review problem.

Options*:
- number talks or number study
- problem of the day
- calendar time
- quick games (for example, Buzz or Around the World)
- discussion of an incorrectly solved problem
- number of the day (use the template on page 183)
- fact fluency practice
- daily review problems

2 Mini-Lesson
10–15 minutes

The mini-lesson is a teacher-led, whole-group activity. This is when new vocabulary and foundational information should be introduced and modeled. Teachers should model math thinking as they work through example problems. Often, students work with a practice problem to clear up any misconceptions.

Options*:
- present a textbook lesson
- show an introduction video
- solve a problem and think aloud
- demonstrate a new strategy
- direct a hands-on activity
- create an anchor chart
- share a math read-aloud
- review the previous day's lesson

*Please note that the options provided are a starting point and there are many more options you can explore for each section.

3 Rotations
10–20 minutes each

Students rotate through guided math with the teacher, independent practice, and workstations. This is also the time when teachers may choose to skip small group instruction in favor of one-on-one conferencing with students.

Guided Math

During this time, you work with small (eight or fewer students), flexible, leveled groups of students to extend and enhance the mini-lesson. Students use manipulatives to better understand the reasoning, procedures, strategies, etc., of the topic. Focus on using math talk and math tools to make sure students really understand the topic. Begin with the lowest group so they do not work on independent practice until after small-group instruction. Like the mini-lesson, these lessons can follow the warm-up/explanation/guided practice/independent practice/assessment model, although they don't have to.

Independent Stations

This segment is also known as centers, rotations, workstations, etc. Activities can be individual, partner, or small group and often include both practice of the current skill or topic and review of past skills. Activities should be introduced ahead of time so students can work independently and should be at a level that won't produce frustration. Students can follow a strict rotation or may be given daily choices as long as they complete certain set activities each week.

Options*:
- math games and activities
- fact fluency practice
- Solve the Room activities
- technology centers (including online games and district-mandated math programs)
- practice sheets (*Note:* The practice sheets included in the lessons are all different, so students can progress through them as they gain understanding of the skill.)
- journaling and/or interactive notebooks

Conferencing

Instead of leading guided math groups, you may choose to periodically observe students during independent stations or pull students for one-on-one conferencing. This allows for formative assessment and more targeted instruction for students who need more help with a skill. This is also an ideal time to do state- or district-mandated quarterly testing.

4 Closure/Reflection
3–5 minutes

The closure is a short, targeted way to wrap up the learning students did during math workshop. It is the perfect time to review the math objective or essential question and answer any questions students may still have.

Options*:
- exit tickets
- allow a few students to explain an "ah-ha!" moment they had
- think/pair/share problem-solving
- math talk prompts
- quick journaling
- students can share what they learned in their own words
- Q and A time

*Please note that the options provided are a starting point and there are many more options you can explore for each section.

What Does Math Workshop Look Like?

Due to the nature of the workshop model, math workshop will look different in different classrooms. You can change it however you need so that it works best for your classroom. See below for ideas and examples of how you can reshape math workshop for your needs.

Timing and Structure
- You can conduct math workshop daily, a few times a week, or monthly.
- Or, you can use one or two days to teach longer whole-class lessons and use the remaining days for rotations.
- Meet with each leveled group daily, or only once or twice a week, depending on how long your math block is.
- Have students visit every station daily or visit each station once each week.

Content
- Use your textbook, a prescribed curriculum, or make your own lessons.
- You can have students use math notebooks for recording work and/or journaling.
- Use the same handful of simple games so you don't have to reinvent the wheel (for example, sorting activities, puzzles, concentration, etc.).
- The lessons provided in this book are interchangeable. If you don't like one or more of the suggestions, replace it with your own.

Assessment
- Build in formal assessment as a longer closure, as a station to visit, or take a day off to administer a test.
- You may choose to have students record the results from each activity or use a checklist during rotations.
- See page 13 for more information on accountability during math workshop.

Grouping
- Groups do not have to be the same size.
- You can have more than one group at the same level to ensure small groups.
- To group students, you can use formative assessment, pretests, or group them on the fly after observations made during the previous day or the mini-lesson.
- You can choose to move students between leveled groups as needed (which could even mean daily) or after more formal assessments.

Choice
- You can require students to visit rotations in a certain order and/or on specific days.
- Or, you can allow students to choose which centers to complete each day.
- You may choose to make students responsible for completing all of the rotations by the end of the week, or you can make some rotations mandatory each day (such as independent practice, fact fluency, and technology centers).
- Students can complete rotations at their desks so you can keep an eye on them, or you can allow them to work in various spots around the room.

Managing Math Workshop

Math workshop can be daunting to newcomers because of all of the elements that need preparation and upkeep. However, the tips and suggestions below for managing the various parts of math workshop will help you get started on the right foot and maintain it throughout the year.

Starting and Maintaining Math Workshop

- Set student expectations before beginning. See page 11 for more information.
- Don't underestimate the power of positive reinforcement.
- Stop and practice the routines and procedures as needed throughout the year if students aren't following expectations.
- Start slow! Begin with only one game or activity during rotations.
- Practice any new games or activities with the whole group first.
- Keep it simple. To begin with, use familiar activities such as concentration, war, or dominoes.
- As you introduce new activities through the year, use the same formats so you don't have to teach a new set of rules each time.
- If possible, use assistants or parent volunteers to monitor students during the first few weeks.
- During weeks with field trips, assemblies, etc., try to move math workshop to a different time. Or, use the entire week to review old concepts and meet with groups that need more help with old concepts instead of introducing a new topic.

Organizing Materials

- Keep all of the necessary supplies in the area where you meet for guided math. That way, students don't waste time looking for materials such as pencils, paper, and manipulatives.
- Use bins or baskets to organize activities, games, and small group supplies for guided math, so everything needed to complete the activity is in one easy-to-grab place.
- Make all math manipulatives visible and accessible so students can use whatever tools they need whenever they need to.
- Make several copies of each activity so multiple pairs or groups of students can work on the same one.
- Designate a student or students each week to be the Materials Master. Their job is to make sure all materials are cleaned up and organized each day.

Managing Math Workshop, cont.

Classroom Management

Managing Rotations

- Use a bulletin board, pocket chart, or interactive whiteboard for a visual reminder of the rotations order. Refer to the example below.
- Use self-stick notes with student names to make reorganizing leveled groups quick and easy.
- Use visual cues and directions on games so students can work independently.
- When students are absent, you can catch them up during conferencing/one-on-one time or temporarily move them to a lower group.

Student Behavior

- For early finishers: have review, extension, or older activities available; make a packet with word problems or challenges to complete; or create a chart listing things they can move on to.
- Foster independence with an "ask three before me" policy.
- Have students use a special hand signal so they can ask to use the bathroom without interrupting guided math.
- For students who have trouble working independently, remove them from rotations and have them sit at a desk near the guided math group until they are ready to rejoin rotations. It may be helpful to have those students start back slowly, with only one independent activity reintroduced at a time.

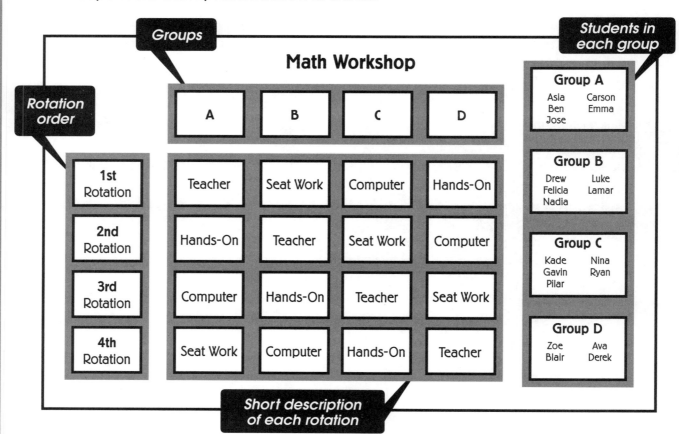

Groups

Students in each group

Math Workshop

	A	B	C	D

Rotation order

1st Rotation	Teacher	Seat Work	Computer	Hands-On
2nd Rotation	Hands-On	Teacher	Seat Work	Computer
3rd Rotation	Computer	Hands-On	Teacher	Seat Work
4th Rotation	Seat Work	Computer	Hands-On	Teacher

Group A
Asia   Carson
Ben   Emma
Jose

Group B
Drew   Luke
Felicia Lamar
Nadia

Group C
Kade   Nina
Gavin   Ryan
Pilar

Group D
Zoe   Ava
Blair   Derek

Short description of each rotation

Planning and Preparation

As with anything, math workshop will be less stressful and have a better chance of success if you plan in advance. Use your district's scope and sequence, textbook curriculum, or similar to plan roughly when and how long to teach each topic. Then, plan the specifics for only a week or two at a time to allow room for remediation or moving on early, depending on what students need. Use the reproducible below to create a high-level plan for a week. Use page 10 to plan more specifically for the guided math groups for that week.

··

Math Workshop

Week of _____

Objective:	Essential Question:

Mini-Lesson		Rotations
Monday		
Tuesday		
Wednesday		
Thursday		
Friday		

Guided Math

Week of _____

Group 1	Level:	Group 2	Level:
Students:		Students:	
Group 3	Level:	**Group 4**	Level:
Students:		Students:	

	Group 1	Group 2	Group 3	Group 4
Monday				
Tuesday				
Wednesday				
Thursday				
Friday				

Student Expectations

Math workshop will not be perfect from the start. It may be a bit chaotic and students may try to play instead of work. But, by setting student expectations early, and with plenty of practice and modeling, math workshop can run smoothly.

Questions to Consider

How should materials be handled? Will there be dedicated students in charge of the materials? Where will they be stored? When can students access them? How and when should cleanup happen? Should there be a one-minute cleanup warning before switching rotations or is cleaning up part of the transition time? Who is responsible for cleaning up common areas?

How and when can students work with others? What activities should be done alone, with a partner, or as group work? Who and when can students ask for help?

What does staying on task mean in math workshop? What level should the volume be? Where should students be working? How should students be accountable for the work they've done? What should the conversations sound like?

What happens if students make mistakes or struggle? Who can they ask for help? What materials and strategies are available if a problem is too hard? Can they skip difficult problems or save them for conferencing?

When is the teacher available? Can students interrupt guided math groups? How can they signal they need to go to the bathroom? What is an appropriate reason to interrupt the teacher? Who else can help students and answer questions?

Setting Expectations

One of the first things you should do when beginning math workshop is to clearly outline the expectations. While you don't have to do this in tandem with making an anchor chart, the visual reminder can be helpful for retaining the expectations as well as serving as a visual reminder throughout the year.

- It can be helpful to frame the expectations simply: What should math workshop look like? What should it sound like? What is the student responsible for? What is the teacher responsible for? Refer to the Questions to Consider in the section above for more specific things to discuss.
- Use the reproducible provided on page 12 for students to complete and keep in their math notebooks or folders. Or, have students and parents sign it as a behavior contract at the beginning of the year. It may be helpful to preprogram the information before copying for students who need it.
- Review the anchor chart often in the first few weeks. Start reviewing it daily before beginning math workshop, and then gradually review it less often as students become more self-reliant.

Don't forget to model, model, model! Be sure to start slow, and practice will make perfect!

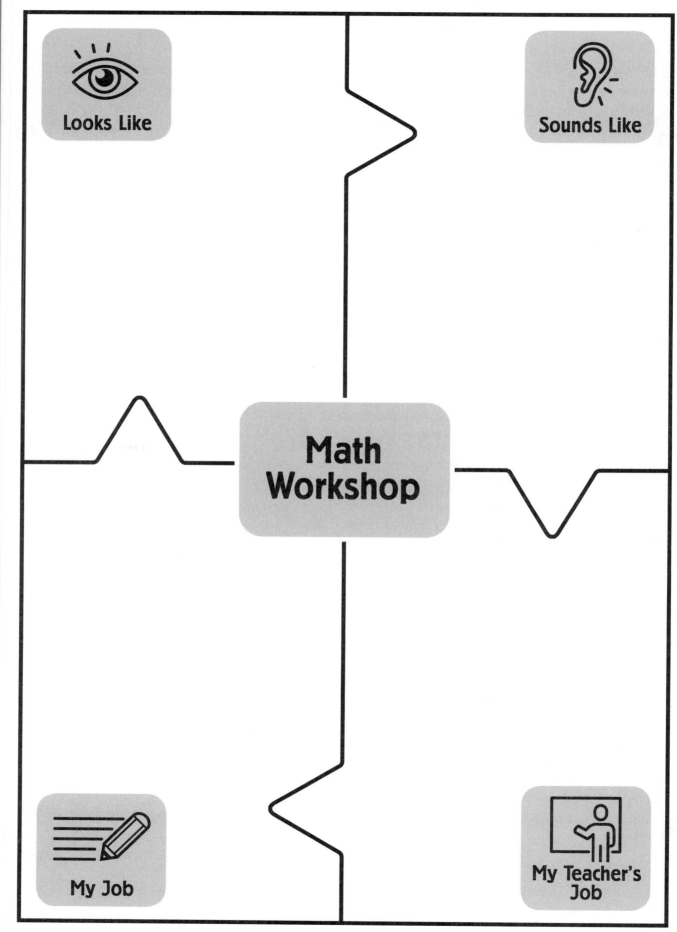

Looks Like

Sounds Like

Math Workshop

My Job

My Teacher's Job

Ensuring Accountability

While moving to a math workshop model has many benefits, it removes the traditional assessment and accountability options in the traditional teaching model. However, it's still necessary to prove in some way that students are working hard toward learning goals and making progress throughout the year. See the lists below for suggestions.

Accountability During Rotations

- Have students record their math thinking (for example, number sentences solved during a game) on whiteboards or something else that is highly visible. That way, you can see at a glance if students are working or not.
- Use activities with recording sheets that you can collect.
- Or, use a recording sheet where students record the rotations they visited and details about their work at each rotation.
- If desired, collect students' written work and/or recording sheets for a participation grade. Use the reproducible on page 14 as a weekly rotation recording sheet or create your own with the rotations specific to your math workshop (see example below).
- Initial, stamp, or sticker students' work daily. You can circulate and do this quickly during closure each day.
- Have students use a math journal to record their work during rotations.
- Utilize technology if possible—many programs and apps have built-in reports on the teacher side.

Assessment

- When not meeting with groups, use the guided math time to visit different stations and have students explain their math thinking for a quick formative assessment.
- During closure, use exit tickets. Use them as formative assessments, or keep them in a math notebook or portfolio to show progress.
- Designate one math workshop day a week or month for a more formal assessment that can be used for a grade or kept in portfolios.

Name_____   Date _____

Math Workshop

Mark off each rotation as you complete it. You must do seat work and technology every day!

Mon	Meet with Teacher	Seat Work	Technology	Fast Practice	Math Game
Tues	Meet with Teacher	Seat Work	Technology	Fast Practice	Math Game
Wed	Meet with Teacher	Seat Work	Technology	Fast Practice	Math Game

Math Rotations

Day	Rotation(s) Visited	Done?	Rate Yourself
Monday			
Tuesday			
Wednesday			
Thursday			
Friday			

1	2	3	4
I didn't do any work. I wasn't on task.	I didn't do my best work and was often off task.	I worked well, but was off task a little.	I worked hard and stayed on task.

Writing Number Sentences

 Essential Question

How are number sentences used to model word problems?

 Warm-Up/Review

Write the terms *sum*, *difference*, *plus*, *minus*, and *equal* on index cards. Divide the class into five groups and distribute an index card and a sheet of white construction paper to each group. Have the groups create representations of their terms, such as number sentences or drawings.

 Mini-Lesson

Materials: several colors of dry-erase markers

1. Draw three squares with one marker and four squares with a different colored marker on the board. Ask, "What does this model show? How many of each color square do you see? What would this model look like using numbers?" Write *3 + 4* under the squares.

2. Ask, "How can you find the answer to this problem? Will the answer be larger or smaller than the numbers in the problem?" Reinforce that addition and multiplication combine groups, while subtraction and division separate groups. Write the sum to complete the number sentence.

3. Draw 10 circles. Then, draw *X*s over 3 of the circles. Ask, "What is this model showing—combining groups or separating them? What do the *X*s mean? What kind of problem does this model show?" Write *10 – 3 = 7* and discuss how each number is expressed in the model.

4. Divide students into pairs. Give each pair a set of counters. Have one student choose an amount of counters and arrange them to show addition or subtraction (for example, a group of counters showing 5 red and 3 yellow could show 5 + 3, 8 – 5, or 8 – 3). Then, the other student should write a related number sentence. Switch and repeat as time allows.

 Math Talk

Explain how you know which operation to use when writing this number sentence.
Tell how you know what number sentence to write.
Why is it important to use the correct operation symbol?

 Journal Prompt

Write a number sentence for each of the following expressions. Then, solve. *five more than six; the difference between seven and one; the sum of three and ten; ten plus nineteen; six less than fourteen*

Materials

index cards with expressions (see below)
linking cubes
cups

 Workstations

Activity sheets (pages 17–19)
Roll-a-Sentence (page 20)

 Guided Math

⚪ **Remediation: Connecting Models and Expressions**

1. Draw 12 bananas and 7 apples. Say, "I want to find the total number of fruits. What kind of problem is this? How can I show it using numbers?"
2. Count the number of bananas and write the total under that fruit. Do the same for the apples. Ask, "Does the word *total* mean addition or subtraction? Which symbol should I use between the numbers?" Write *12 + 7* and find the total by counting all of the fruit.
3. Ask, "How many bananas do I have? If I eat 3 bananas on the way home from the store, how can I show that in my model? (Cross off 3 bananas.) How can I find the total number of bananas I have now? What would that look like in numbers?" Write *12 – 3* and demonstrate how to find the difference.
4. Write addition and subtraction expressions on index cards. Have students choose expressions and draw the matching models.

🔲 **On Level: Number Sentences**

1. Explain to students that they can use pictures, objects, models, or drawings to help them solve problems. Sometimes, seeing a problem in a different way can make the answer easier to find.
2. Draw 6 shaded circles and 8 unshaded circles. Ask, "What does this model show? What would this model look like using numbers?" Write *6 + 8 = 14* under the problem. Have students verify the answer by counting the circles.
3. Draw a set of 14 circles. Draw Xs over 6 of the circles. Ask, "What kind of problem does this model show? What do the Xs mean? What does this look like as a number sentence?" Write *14 – 6 = 8*. Have students verify the answer using the model.
4. Look at the 6 shaded circles and 8 unshaded circles again. Ask, "What is a different way this shows a subtraction problem? How many more circles are unshaded than shaded?" Write *8 – 6 = 2*.
5. Have students draw models and write the matching math sentences.

🔺 **Enrichment: Modeling Multiple Equations**

1. Place an array of two different colors of linking cubes on a table (for example, 7 red and 13 blue arranged in 4 rows of 5). Ask, "What equation does this model show?" Accept all suggestions that are mathematically sound. (For example, red cubes plus blue cubes, blue cubes minus red cubes, repeated addition of 5 or 4, or multiplication of 4 rows of 5 cubes.)
2. Write all of the equations and discuss how they each represent the model.
3. Allow students to experiment with unit cubes. Provide empty cups for addition, grouping, or subtraction. For example, a student may start with a group of 12, and place 3 in a cup to demonstrate subtraction.
4. Have students draw sketches of their models and write the matching number sentences.

 Assess and Extend

Write several number sentences on the board. Have students draw models to express the number sentences.

Writing Number Sentences

Draw lines to match each model to the number sentence. Solve.

1.

A. $5 + 3 =$ _____

2.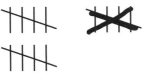

B. $24 - 8 =$ _____

3.

C. $6 + 5 =$ _____

4.

D. $8 + 8 =$ _____

5.

E. $15 - 5 =$ _____

6.

F. $9 - 4 =$ _____

Writing Number Sentences

Write a number sentence for each model. Solve.

1. ⊗⊗⊗⊗⊗⊗⊗⊗○○○○○○   _____

2. ■■■■■■□□□□□   _____

3. ✕✕✕✕△△△△△△△△   _____

4. ☆☆☆☆★★★★★★★   _____

5. ⬠⬠⬠⬠⬠⬠⬠⬠⬠⬠   _____

Write a number sentence for each word problem. Draw a picture to solve.

6. Marcus had 17 trading cards. He gave 9 of them to his little brother. How many trading cards does Marcus have left?

7. A waitress made 15 side salads during lunch and 12 more during dinner. How many side salads did she make in all?

8. Nicole has 14 sunflowers to plant. She planted 8 of the flowers. How many more sunflowers does Nicole have left to plant?

Writing Number Sentences   ▲ Modeling Multiple Equations

Write two different number sentences for each model. Solve.

1.

_____   _____

2.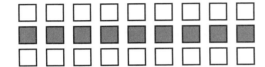

_____   _____

3.

_____   _____

4.

_____   _____

Write a number sentence for each word problem. Solve.

5. There are 28 student desks in a classroom. The teacher wants to put the desks into 4 equal rows. How many desks will go in each row?

_____

6. Ben raked and filled 8 bags of leaves. Each bag weighed 10 pounds. How many total pounds of leaves did Ben rake?

_____

Roll-a-Sentence

Materials: two-color counters

To play: Grab a handful of counters. Drop them gently. Write the related number sentence. For example, you could add the amount of yellow and red counters, or subtract the amount of yellow or red counters from the total. Draw a model. Solve.

I. _____ ◯ _____ = _____	**2.** _____ ◯ _____ = _____
3. _____ ◯ _____ = _____	**4.** _____ ◯ _____ = _____
5. _____ ◯ _____ = _____	**6.** _____ ◯ _____ = _____
7. _____ ◯ _____ = _____	**8.** _____ ◯ _____ = _____

Solving Word Problems

 Essential Question

How can addition and subtraction be used to solve word problems?

 Warm-Up/Review

Write the following word problem on the board: *Seventeen birds were sitting on a fence. Seven of the birds flew away. How many birds are left on the fence?* Have students solve it with a partner and share their answers. Discuss the different strategies students used to solve the problem.

 Mini-Lesson

Materials: copies of word problems (see below), highlighters

1. Display or provide copies of the following problem: *Last year, Andrea got 15 presents for her birthday. Today, Andrea got 12 presents for her birthday. She has opened 7 of the presents. How many more presents does she have left to open?*

2. Read the problem aloud. Ask students to highlight or circle all of the numbers in the problem. Have them study the numbers and place an *X* on the numbers they do not need. (15) Explain that this information is not necessary to solve the problem.

3. Ask, "Is this an addition or a subtraction problem? How do you know?" Have them highlight or circle the key word that gives a clue to which operation to use. (*left*) Discuss the context of the problem and how it also points to using subtraction.

4. Model how to draw a picture to represent the problem.

5. Write a number sentence and solve for the answer. Ask students if the answer makes sense and discuss why or why not.

6. Have pairs of students work together to solve the following problem using the above steps: *Dante has 9 action figures and Jose has 8. Dante also has 3 toy cars. How many action figures do they have altogether?* Allow students to share their answers and strategies.

 Math Talk

What key words did you notice in the word problem?
What strategy did you use to solve the word problem?
Could you have used another type of strategy? Which one?

 Journal Prompt

Which strategy (drawing a picture, using numbers, acting it out, etc.) are you most comfortable using to solve a word problem? Why?

Materials

copies of word problems (see below)
highlighters
linking cubes

 Workstations

Activity sheets (pages 23–25)
Word Problem Poke Cards
(page 26)

 Guided Math

○ **Remediation: Modeling Word Problems**

1. Read the word problem: *Ivan has 4 red cars and 7 yellow cars. How many cars does Ivan have altogether?* Provide a copy to each student.

2. Explain, "Before starting any word problem, figure out what you are trying to solve for." Identify and highlight the question. Model how to reword the question into a statement. (*Ivan has ___ cars altogether.*)

3. Ask, "Is this an addition or a subtraction problem? How can we use the context of the word problem to find out?" Highlight the key word. (*altogether*) Then, have students find and highlight the numbers needed to solve the problem.

4. Connect 4 red linking cubes and 7 yellow linking cubes to model the problem. Write *4 + 7 = __*. Count the cubes to solve the problem and fill in the blank. Then ask, "Is there another way to solve this problem?" Have students come up with other strategies, such as drawing a model.

5. Continue with visual, concrete examples with other word problems. Encourage students to identify the question, identify key words and numbers, and use a model.

▢ **On Level: Word Problems with Unknowns**

1. Read the word problem: *Jill baked 34 muffins. She gave some muffins to her friends. Jill had 20 muffins left. How many muffins did she give to her friends?* Provide a copy to each student.

2. Have students use highlighters to identify the question and use it to frame the answer they are looking for. (*Jill gave away ___ muffins.*)

3. Ask, "Do we know how many muffins Jill started with? Use the linking cubes (or other manipulatives, number lines, or drawings) to show me how many muffins she baked." Check students' work for accuracy.

4. Ask, "How many muffins did Jill have left at the end of the story? Use the cubes to show me. Can you tell me how many muffins she gave away?" Write the number sentence *34 – ? = 20*. Explain, "We can use a symbol or a box to represent the unknown number in this problem." Have students use their manipulatives to find the answer. (*14*)

5. Continue practicing with other word problems with unknowns in all positions.

△ **Enrichment: Labeling Information in Multi-Step Word Problems**

1. Read the word problem: *Javon's mom gave him $90 to spend on clothes. He bought a shirt for $18, a hat for $10, and jeans for $26. How much money does Javon have left?* Provide a copy to each student.

2. Have students use highlighters to identify the question and use it to frame the answer they are looking for. (*Javon has $__ left.*) Then, have students circle the key information in the problem. Explain that context is important. Have students volunteer what operations they think they should perform and why.

3. Have students solve the problem and share their solutions. Connect the operations they chose to use with phrases used in the word problem. (*and*: addition; *have left*: subtraction)

4. Continue practicing with other multi-step word problems. Encourage students to justify the operations they choose and the order they perform the steps.

 Assess and Extend

Write a word problem on the board and have students solve it. Then, have students explain the steps they took to solve it.

Solving Word Problems   ● Modeling Word Problems

Read each problem. Highlight key words. Draw a picture to solve.
Write the number sentence.

1. Ellis picks 9 flowers. He put 4 of the flowers in a vase. How many flowers does he have left?	**2.** Mr. Novak put 12 grapes in his fruit salad. Then, he added 5 cherries. How many pieces of fruit did he put in altogether?

____ ◯ ____ ◯ ____   ____ ◯ ____ ◯ ____

3. Fiona has 6 cows and 12 chickens on her farm. How many more chickens does she have than cows?	**4.** Daysha has 13 beads. She uses 11 beads to make a bracelet. How many beads does she have left?

____ ◯ ____ ◯ ____   ____ ◯ ____ ◯ ____

Solving Word Problems ▪ Word Problems with Unknowns

Read each problem. Highlight key words. Write a number sentence with a question mark (?) to show the missing addend. Solve the problem.

1. Julio collected 16 shells. He found 5 white shells. The rest of the shells were brown. How many of the shells were brown?

_____ + _____ = _____

_____ brown shells

2. Twenty-six students are in Mrs. Gladd's class. Fifteen students turned in homework. How many students did not turn in homework?

_____ + _____ = _____

_____ students

3. Tony collected 7 trading cards. Yasmin collected more trading cards than Tony. In all, they have 22 trading cards. How many trading cards does Yasmin have?

_____ + _____ = _____

_____ trading cards

4. Alexa picked 16 flowers on Friday. On Saturday, she picked some more flowers. Now, she has 24 flowers. How many flowers did Alexa pick on Saturday?

_____ + _____ = _____

_____ flowers

5. Forrest read 30 pages of his book today. He read some pages before lunch. He read 13 pages before bedtime. How many pages of his book did he read today?

_____ + _____ = _____

_____ pages

6. Evan dropped 55 marbles on the floor. He picked up 30 of them. Cindy picked up the rest of them. How many marbles did Cindy pick up?

_____ + _____ = _____

_____ marbles

Solving Word Problems

▲ Labeling Information in Multi-Step Word Problems

Read each problem. Highlight the question and circle key words. Complete the statements. Solve.

---

1. Sasha's class made 46 hearts to decorate the classroom. They put 22 on the windows and 12 on the door. How many hearts do they have left to use?

First, I will _____.

Then, I will _____.

_____ hearts

---

2. Zack's mother baked 27 cupcakes yesterday and 24 today. Zack and his sister and brother ate 11 of them. How many cupcakes are left?

First, I will _____.

Then, I will _____.

_____ cupcakes

---

3. At an amusement park, Brianna wants to ride a roller coaster that costs 27 tickets and a merry-go-round that costs 20 tickets. She has 35 tickets. How many more tickets does she need?

First, I will _____.

Then, I will _____.

_____ tickets

---

4. Felipe collects coins. He got 30 coins from his brother, 23 coins from his mother, and 31 coins from his uncle. He lost 25 coins. How many coins does he have in his piggy bank now?

First, I will _____.

Then, I will _____.

_____ coins

Word Problem Poke Cards

To play: Choose a card and solve the word problem. Then, poke a pencil through the hole you think is the correct answer. To check, turn the card over and see if your pencil is inserted through the circled hole.

A bus has 15 students riding on it. At the first bus stop, 7 students get off. How many students are left on the bus? 5 8 9 ● ● ● **A**	David has 22 more toy cars than Luke. David has 48 toy cars. How many toy cars does Luke have? 63 53 26 ● ● ● **B**
Mr. Adams placed 28 crackers on a plate. Megan ate 5 crackers. Then, Abe ate 2 crackers. How many crackers are left on the plate? 21 22 31 ● ● ● **C**	Lynn has 23 bows. Her mom gives her 11 more. How many bows does Lynn have now? 12 22 34 ● ● ● **D**
Miguel is on a team with 35 students. There are 20 girls on the team. How many boys are on the team? 10 25 15 ● ● ● **E**	Blake's dad puts 56 grapes in a bag. Blake eats 25 of them. How many grapes are left now? 31 41 25 ● ● ● **F**
Ms. Parker bought 39 cherry tomatoes. She used 22 of them in salads. How many cherry tomatoes does she have left? 19 17 61 ● ● ● **G**	Matt put 28 red and yellow flowers in a vase. There are 11 red flowers. How many of the flowers are yellow? 17 27 7 ● ● ● **H**

To prep: Copy on card stock and laminate for durability. Cut out the cards. Use a hole punch to punch a hole over the black circles on each card. Then, use a permanent marker to circle the correct hole on the back of the card. Cut off these directions before copying.

Even and Odd Numbers

 ## Essential Question

What makes a number odd or even?

Warm-Up/Review

Have a group of 10 students line up in pairs at the door. Ask, "Does everyone in line have a partner?" Have the students sit down. Then, call on 15 students to line up in pairs at the door. Ask the question again. Explain that the student without a partner is the "odd man out" and 15 is an odd number.

 ## Mini-Lesson

Materials: linking cubes, number line, hundred charts

1. Give each student a handful of linking cubes. Tell students to count out 8 cubes and line them up in equal groups of two. Ask if there are any cubes left over. Explain that 8 is an even number because each cube has a partner.

2. Then, ask students to count out 11 cubes and line them up in equal groups of two. Ask if there are any cubes left over. Explain that 11 is an odd number because one of the cubes does not have a partner. Have students count out other numbers and volunteer whether they are even or odd.

3. Use a number line to illustrate how even and odd numbers skip count by 2s.

4. Using a number line, start at 0 and skip count to 40. Ask, "What do you notice about even numbers?" Point to the pattern in the ones place. Start at 1 and repeat with odd numbers. Ask, "Do the groups share any common numbers in the ones place? Why not?" Point out that even numbers always end in 0, 2, 4, 6, or 8, while odd numbers always end in 1, 3, 5, 7, or 9.

5. Have students practice skip counting forward and backward by 2s, starting at different numbers. Use a number line or a hundred chart as a visual reference.

 ## Math Talk

Explain how you know if _____ is odd or even.
How can pairing or counting by twos help you decide whether a number is odd or even?
What strategy did you use to determine whether the number was odd or even?

 ## Journal Prompt

Make a list of things that come in even numbers, such as mittens or slices of a whole pizza. Can you think of something that comes in an odd number?

Materials

two-color counters
copies of a hundred chart
number line
chart paper
crayons

 Workstations

Activity sheets (pages 29–31)
Spin-and-Fill (page 32)

 Guided Math

◯ **Remediation: Reinforcing Patterns**

1. Review the terms *even* and *odd*. Give examples of each. Reinforce the concept of skip counting as counting in groups. Demonstrate skip counting by 2s by moving pairs of counters as you say each number, and on a hundred chart as you count aloud.

2. Start at 2. Mark all of the even numbers on a number line with the same color counter. Say them aloud together as you point to each one. Ask, "What numbers are skipped? Why?"

3. Leave the even counters in place. Start at 1 and mark all of the odd numbers with counters showing the other color. Say them aloud together as you point to each one.

4. Ask, "How can you tell whether a number is even or odd?" Discuss the pattern of numbers in the ones place for both kinds of numbers. Write several numbers on chart paper. Ask students to classify each number as even or odd based on the digit in the ones place.

5. Then, have students give examples of even and odd numbers.

◻ **On Level: Practicing Skip Counting**

1. Use a hundred chart and counters as a visual reference of odds and evens. Give each student crayons and a copy of a hundred chart. Have students start at 2 and color all of the even numbers on their charts. Ask, "What is an even number? How can you tell whether a number is even?" Repeat with odd numbers using a different color.

2. Ask, "What digits are in the ones place in even numbers? Odd numbers? Is that always true, even for very large numbers? How do you know?"

3. Start on the number *24*. Then, give directions for skip counting. For example, "Start at 24. Skip count backward by 2s five numbers." Ask, "What is the number?" (14) Follow the same process with other even and odd numbers, giving directions to skip count forward and backward.

4. Have students write skip-counting riddles. Allow students to share their riddles with partners to solve.

▲ **Enrichment: Identifying Multiples of Two**

1. Brainstorm everyday objects that come in pairs. Discuss the ease of counting a large quantity of any of these things using multiples of 2. Ask questions like, "How many socks are 5 people wearing? How many gloves are 12 children wearing?" Have students skip count by 2s to determine the answers.

2. Challenge students to give examples of very large numbers that are multiples of 2. Reinforce the pattern of looking at the ones place to determine whether a number is even or odd.

3. Discuss multiples of other numbers, such as 10, 5, and 3. Use a hundred chart to mark the multiples and investigate where numbers overlap categories and why.

4. Have students discuss the question, "If you can skip count by 2 along odd numbers, why are odd numbers not multiples of 2?" (Because you are not starting with the number 2.)

 Assess and Extend

Display a list of numbers, such as *10, 18, 11, 6,* and *13*. Have students tell whether each number is odd or even and explain their reasoning.

Even and Odd Numbers   ● Reinforcing Patterns

Start at 16. Skip count by 2s in order. Color each even number yellow to create a path. You can move up, down, across, or diagonally.

Start 16	18	19	21	23
17	20	22	24	35
15	29	27	26	30
23	32	28	25	32
34	30	39	37	30
36	38	40	42	44

Even and Odd Numbers

Start with the first number in each row. Skip count by 2s. Write the numbers in order on the lines. Then, tell whether the numbers are *even* or *odd*.

	Skip Count	**Even or Odd**
1. 48	_____ _____ _____ _____	_____
2. 35	_____ _____ _____ _____	_____
3. 20	_____ _____ _____ _____	_____
4. 73	_____ _____ _____ _____	_____
5. 64	_____ _____ _____ _____	_____
6. 9	_____ _____ _____ _____	_____
7. 81	_____ _____ _____ _____	_____
8. 92	_____ _____ _____ _____	_____

Skip count by 2s to follow the directions.

9. Counting forward, write all of the odd numbers between 18 and 31.

_____

10. Counting backward, write all of the even numbers between 109 and 95.

_____

11. Counting backward, write all of the odd numbers between 60 and 49.

_____

12. Counting forward, write all of the even numbers between 43 and 57.

_____

Even and Odd Numbers   ▲ Identifying Multiples of Two

Each list skip counts by 2s. Circle the number in each list that is not correct. Write the correct number. Then, write *yes* or *no* to show if the numbers are multiples of 2.

		Correct Number	Multiple of 2?
1.	86, 85, 82, 80, 78, 76, 74, 72	_____	_____
2.	19, 21, 23, 25, 28, 29, 31, 33	_____	_____
3.	42, 44, 46, 48, 51, 52, 54, 56	_____	_____
4.	103, 101, 98, 97, 95, 93, 91, 89	_____	_____
5.	58, 60, 62, 63, 66, 68, 70, 72	_____	_____
6.	914, 916, 918, 920, 922, 924, 927	_____	_____

Read each problem. Answer the question. Draw a picture to show your work.

7. Each car has 2 headlights. There are 7 cars in a parking lot. How many total headlights are there?

8. Allie folds 12 pairs of socks. How many socks are there in all?

9. A store orders 19 pairs of new tennis shoes. How many total shoes are ordered?

Spin-and-Fill

Materials: sharpened pencil, paper clip, two colors of counters

To play: Players take turns. Use the sharpened pencil and paper clip to spin the spinner. If the spinner lands on Even, place the counter on an even number on the board. If the spinner lands on Odd, place the counter on an odd number on the board. If a counter is already on a space, a player may not place another counter on it. If a player cannot place a counter on a space, he loses a turn. Continue playing until the board is filled. The player with the most counters on the board wins the game. Repeat for Round 2.

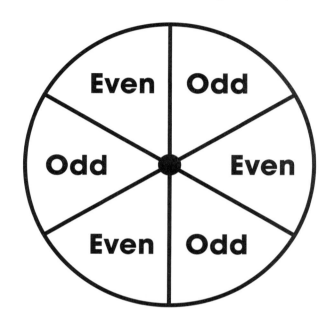

Round 1

22	15	17	5	98	16	14
10	2	65	33	9	72	27

Round 2

19	8	58	62	71	28	55
96	11	40	12	31	83	39

 **Patterning**

 Essential Question

How are number or shape patterns related to equations?

 Warm-Up/Review

Draw a pattern of alternating circles, stars, and diamonds. Have students name the shapes aloud, starting at the left and moving right. Ask whether they notice a part that repeats. Explain that patterns repeat. Have a student come to the board and circle the set of objects that repeats.

 Mini-Lesson

Materials: number lines, counters

1. Give each student a number line and counters. Write the following list of numbers on the board: *4, 7, 10, 13, 16, 19*. Have students mark each number on the number line with a counter. Ask, "Do the numbers get larger or smaller? Do they change by the same amount each time?"

2. Model how to find the difference between the first pair of numbers in the list. Then, check the difference between each consecutive pair. Tell students that the numbers in the list increase by 3. Demonstrate how to extend the pattern by adding 3 and writing the next several numbers. (22, 25, 28, etc.)

3. Repeat step 1 with the numbers *22, 20, 18, 16,* and *14*. Reinforce that moving to the left on a number line means subtraction (getting smaller), and moving to the right means addition (getting larger).

4. Discuss the number pattern together. Have students use counters on the number line to find the next three numbers.

5. Have pairs of students work together to create their own number patterns and identify the pattern.

 Math Talk

How are number patterns like skip counting? What is the next number? How do you know? What is the rule for this pattern?

 Journal Prompt

How can finding number patterns help you solve problems? Provide an example.

Materials

number lines

 Workstations

Activity sheets (pages 35–37)
Caterpillars Rule! (page 38)

 Guided Math

⬤ **Remediation: Practicing Number Patterns**

1. Ask, "What is a pattern? Do patterns have to use pictures? What number patterns do you know?" Give examples of familiar patterns (2s, 5s, 10s, 100s).
2. Write the following numbers: 9, 11, 13, 15, 17. Ask, "Do the numbers get larger or smaller? Do they change by the same amount each time? What is the pattern rule?" Explain that the pattern by which the numbers increase or decrease is called the *pattern rule*.
3. Write the following: 4, ____, 12, ____, 20, 24. Call on volunteers to fill in the blanks to complete the pattern. If needed, mark the known numbers on a number line and identify the rule.
4. Repeat this process with a subtraction number pattern. (For example, 24, ____, 18, ____, 12)
5. Review how to use the number line to emphasize the concept of addition (moving to the right) and subtraction (moving to the left).
6. Write several more number patterns on the board with missing numbers. Have students copy them and fill in the missing numbers.

⬛ **On Level: Identifying Number Patterns**

1. Ask, "Can you think of number patterns in your everyday life?" (For example, days in a week, months in a year, years in a decade, minutes in an hour, hours in a day, numerals on a clock, inches in a foot, feet in a mile) Identify the repeating pattern in each example.
2. Write the following numbers on the board: 15, 22, 29, 36, 43, 50. Ask, "Are the numbers getting larger or smaller by the same amount each time? What is the pattern rule for this group of numbers? (+7) What would be the next number in the pattern?" Follow the same process for a subtraction sequence.
3. Write the following numbers: 2, 7, 9, 10, 13, 17. Ask, "Are the numbers getting larger or smaller? Do they change by the same amount each time? (No) Is there a way to predict what number will come next? (No) Is there a pattern here? (No)"
4. Have students write number patterns and exchange with partners to identify them.

▲ **Enrichment: Growing Number Patterns**

1. Challenge students with an example of a pattern that changes by a different amount each time, but in a predictable way. For example, 1, 2, 4, 7, 11, 16, 22 (+1, +2, +3, +4, +5, +6) or 90, 85, 75, 60 (-5, -10, -15). Discuss how to find the sum or difference between consecutive numbers. Ask, "How do the numbers change each time?"
2. Explain that the difference between each pair of consecutive numbers is a pattern in itself. Ask, "What is the pattern for creating this group of numbers? How can we extend the pattern?" Follow the same process for a subtraction sequence.
3. Invite students to create their own growing patterns. Emphasize that the pattern has to be consistent so it is recognizable. Have students identify and extend each number pattern example.
4. Have students discuss the importance of consistency in identifying a pattern in a list of numbers.

 Assess and Extend

Provide a hundred chart to each student. Have them identify a pattern. Students should give the first 10 numbers in the pattern and explain the pattern using words and/or a number sentence.

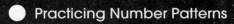

Patterning   ● Practicing Number Patterns

Write the next three numbers in each pattern. Use the number line to help you.

0 1 2 3 4 5 6 7 8 9 10 11 12 13 14 15 16 17 18 19 20 21 22 23 24 25 26 27 28 29 30

1. 3, 6, 9, 12, 15, _____ , _____ , _____

2. 1, 5, 9, 13, 17, _____ , _____ , _____

3. 17, 15, 13, 11, 9, _____ , _____ , _____

4. 45, 40, 35, 30, 25, _____ , _____ , _____

5. 8, 10, 12, 14, 16, _____ , _____ , _____

6. 2, 8, 14, 20, 26, _____ , _____ , _____

7. 33, 29, 25, 21, 17, _____ , _____ , _____

8. 6, 11, 16, 21, 26, _____ , _____ , _____

9. 28, 25, 22, 19, 16, _____ , _____ , _____

10. 45, 39, 33, 27, 21, _____ , _____ , _____

+÷-× Patterning   ■ Identifying Number Patterns

Identify the pattern in each series of numbers. Write the next number in the pattern.

1. 21, 23, 25, 27, 29, _____   Pattern: _____

2. 36, 33, 30, 27, 24, _____   Pattern: _____

3. 1, 7, 13, 19, 25, _____   Pattern: _____

4. 42, 38, 34, 30, 26, _____   Pattern: _____

5. 3, 8, 13, 18, 23, _____   Pattern: _____

6. 24, 34, 44, 54, 64, _____   Pattern: _____

7. 64, 56, 48, 40, 32, _____   Pattern: _____

8. 91, 82, 73, 64, 55, _____   Pattern: _____

9. 13, 25, 37, 49, 61, _____   Pattern: _____

10. 101, 86, 71, 56, _____   Pattern: _____

11. 82, 75, 68, 61, 54, _____   Pattern: _____

12. 17, 40, 63, 86, 109, _____   Pattern: _____

Patterning   ▲ Growing Number Patterns

Write the missing numbers in each pattern. Then, write the rule.

1. 33, 37, _____, 45, 49, 53, _____, _____   _____

2. _____, 24, 22, _____, 18, 16, 14, _____   _____

3. 11, 20, 29, 38, _____, 56, _____, _____   _____

4. 36, _____, 56, 66, 76, _____, _____, 106   _____

5. 97, 94, 91, _____, 85, 82, _____, _____   _____

6. _____, _____, _____, 32, 26, 20, 14   _____

7. 15, _____, 31, 39, 47, _____, _____, 71   _____

Find each pattern. Write the next three numbers.

8. 2, 4, 8, 14, 22, _____, _____, _____

9. 52, 51, 48, 43, 36, _____, _____, _____

10. 200, 195, 185, 170, 150, _____, _____, _____

11. 1, 4, 10, 19, 31, 46, _____, _____, _____

12. 23, 24, 26, 29, 33, _____, _____, _____

Caterpillars Rule!

Materials: 1 die or number cube
To play: Roll the die and record the number in the box on the left. This number will be the "rule." Then, look at the "Start" number and continue the number pattern by adding (or subtracting) the rule to or from it. Record the rule on the caterpillar's head.

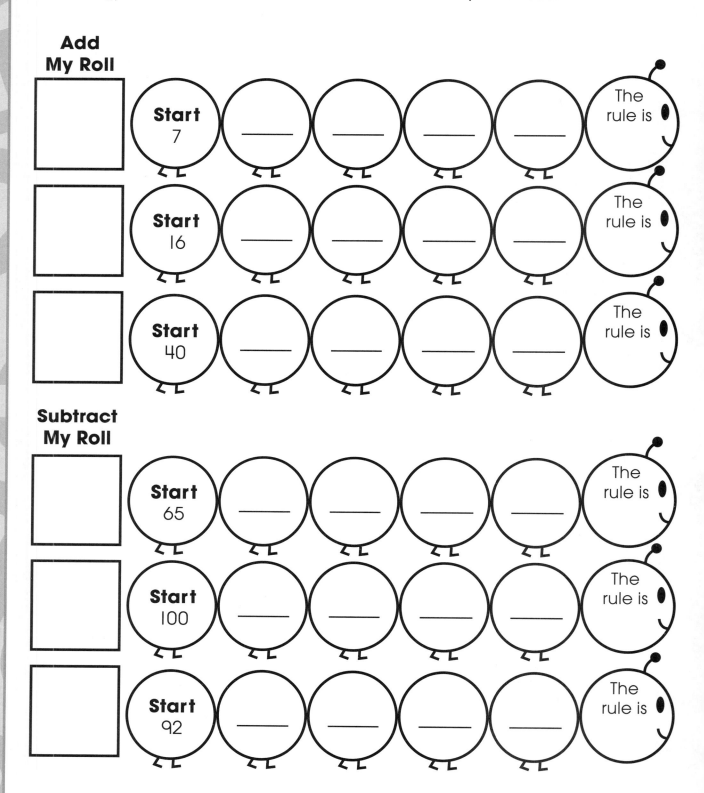

**Add
My Roll**

Start 7 ___ ___ ___ ___ The rule is

Start 16 ___ ___ ___ ___ The rule is

Start 40 ___ ___ ___ ___ The rule is

**Subtract
My Roll**

Start 65 ___ ___ ___ ___ The rule is

Start 100 ___ ___ ___ ___ The rule is

Start 92 ___ ___ ___ ___ The rule is

 **Arrays**

 Essential Question

How can using repeated addition help to count a group?

 Warm-Up/Review

To review columns and rows have students stand up straight by their desks. Remind them that this is how a column goes: straight up and down, vertically. Then, have students lay down straight on the floor or carpet. Explain how this is the way a row goes: straight across, horizontally.

 Mini-Lesson

Materials: sticky notes, linking cubes

1. Introduce the term *array* as a group of items arranged in rows and columns. Then, place 5 sets of 2 sticky notes in an array on the board. Ask, "How many pairs of notes are there?" Refer to one of the pairs as a set. Ask, "How many notes are in each set? How many sets are there?" (There are 5 equal sets of 2.)

2. Ask, "What could I do to find the total number of notes? How can I write that as an addition sentence?" Write *2 + 2 + 2 + 2 + 2 = 10* on the board. Explain that sometimes the number of objects in a set is quite large or you have many sets, so adding to find the total can take too long.

3. Define multiplication as a quicker way to add many sets of the same size. Remind students that the model shows 5 equal sets of 2. Write the multiplication sentence *5 × 2 = 10*. Read the sentence as "5 groups of 2 notes in each set equals 10 total notes" or "5 times 2 equals 10."

4. Repeat steps 1–3 with 3 sets of 4 sticky notes. Guide students to identify the addition (4 + 4 + 4) and multiplication (3 × 4) sentences shown by the model.

5. Distribute linking cubes to pairs of students. Have them practice sorting the linking cubes into arrays. Then, they should write the related addition and multiplication sentences.

Note: This lesson does not correlate rows and columns with a specific order for the factors in the related multiplcation sentence. This is done to better prepare students to understand the Commutative Property of Multiplication. If desired, the lesson can be easily adjusted to teach that the rows and columns in an array should be used in a specific order.

 Math Talk

How does repeated addition help you understand multiplication?
How are addition and multiplication related?
Why does multiplication make it easier to count a large number of objects?

 Journal Prompt

Draw examples of arrays in the real world. Write an addition and multiplication sentence for the array in each example.

Materials

linking cubes
graph paper

 Workstations

Activity sheets (pages 41–43)
Array Punch (page 44)

 Guided Math

⬤ **Remediation: Using Arrays to Add**

1. Organize linking cubes into 5 sets of 4. Ask, "How many sets are there? How many cubes are in one set? Do all of the sets have the same number of cubes?"

2. Ask students how they could find the total number of cubes using addition. Help them write *4 + 4 + 4 + 4 + 4 = 20*. Point out that there are 4 cubes in each set and 5 equal sets. So, they need to add 5 sets of 4 to find the total number.

3. Group cubes in different amounts. Have students point to each set as they say, for example, "3 plus 3 plus 3 plus 3" to write a repeated addition sentence. Show students how to count the cubes in the first set and say "3 times," then count the number of sets and say "1, 2, 3, 4" to introduce writing a multiplication sentence.

◻ **On Level: Focusing on Sets**

1. Use linking cubes to build equal sets. Show students 4 sets of 7 cubes. (*Note*: Use 4 sets of 5 cubes instead if needed to remain within the arrays specified by your state's standards.) Ask, "How many cubes are in each set? How many sets do you have? What two related addition sentences could you write? What two numbers would you write in the multiplication sentence?"

2. Have students count by 7s as they point to each set to find the total number of cubes. Ask a volunteer to write the multiplication sentence *4 x 7 = 28*. Read the sentence as "4 sets of 7 equals 28." Tell students that the multiplication sign is another way of saying "sets of."

3. Arrange cubes into different groups. Continue saying "sets of" to emphasize the equal groupings. Have students write the multiplication sentence for each arrangement.

4. Challenge students to arrange the same number of cubes in different numbers of sets. Ask, "How does the number of cubes in each set change? Is the total still the same?"

△ **Enrichment: Multiplication Arrays**

1. Distribute graph paper to students. On the graph paper, color 3 rows of 7 squares. (*Note*: Use 4 rows of 5 instead if needed to remain within the arrays specified by your state's standards.) Ask, "How many rows are colored? Is there an equal number of squares in each row?"

2. Ask, "How many squares are colored altogether? How can I write this array as a repeated addition sentence? How can I write it as a multiplication sentence?" Read the problem as "3 sets of 7 equals 21."

3. Arrange students in pairs and give each pair 32 cubes. Challenge them to arrange the cubes in arrays. Remind students that there must be an equal number of cubes in each row and column. Have them write a multiplication problem for each array.

4. Have students record their arrays on graph paper and label each array with the corresponding multiplication sentence.

 Assess and Extend

Have students make their own arrays with up to 25 linking cubes. Students should write two related addition sentences to match each array. Challenge students to write the related multiplication sentence.

Arrays

Add the objects in each column to find the total.

1. ✕ ✕ ✕ ✕
✕ ✕ ✕ ✕

$2 + 2 + 2 + 2 =$ ____

2. ◯ ◯ ◯ ◯
◯ ◯ ◯ ◯
◯ ◯ ◯ ◯
◯ ◯ ◯ ◯
◯ ◯ ◯ ◯

$5 + 5 + 5 + 5 =$ ____

Write the repeated addition sentence. Then, solve.

3. ☆ ☆ ☆ ☆ ☆ ☆ ☆

____ + ____ + ____ + ____ +

____ + ____ + ____ = ____

4. ☺ ☺ ☺ ☺ ☺
☺ ☺ ☺ ☺ ☺
☺ ☺ ☺ ☺ ☺

____ + ____ + ____ +

____ + ____ = ____

5. ✕ ✕ ✕ ✕
✕ ✕ ✕ ✕
✕ ✕ ✕ ✕
✕ ✕ ✕ ✕

____ + ____ +

____ + ____ = ____

6. ◯ ◯ ◯ ◯
◯ ◯ ◯ ◯
◯ ◯ ◯ ◯

____ + ____ + ____ + ____ = ____

 **Arrays**   ☐ Focusing on Sets

Look at each array. Write the equal sets. Then, write the multiplication sentence.

1. ○ ○ ○
○ ○ ○

_____ sets of _____

_____ × _____ = _____

2. ☐ ☐ ☐ ☐
☐ ☐ ☐ ☐

_____ sets of _____

_____ × _____ = _____

3. ○ ○ ○ ○ ○
○ ○ ○ ○ ○
○ ○ ○ ○ ○

_____ sets of _____

_____ × _____ = _____

4. ♡ ♡ ♡ ♡
♡ ♡ ♡ ♡

_____ sets of _____

_____ × _____ = _____

5. ♡ ♡ ♡ ♡
♡ ♡ ♡ ♡
♡ ♡ ♡ ♡

_____ sets of _____

_____ × _____ = _____

6. △ △ △ △ △

_____ set of _____

_____ × _____ = _____

7. ☾☾ ☾☾ ☾☾ ☾☾ ☾☾
☾☾ ☾☾ ☾☾ ☾☾ ☾☾

_____ sets of _____

_____ × _____ = _____

8. ☆ ☆ ☆ ☆ ☆
☆ ☆ ☆ ☆ ☆

_____ sets of _____

_____ × _____ = _____

Arrays

Look at each array. Write the repeated addition sentence. Then, write the multiplication sentence.

1.

_____ = ____

____ × ____ = ____

2.

_____ = ____

____ × ____ = ____

3.

_____ = ____

____ × ____ = ____

4.

_____ = ____

____ × ____ = ____

5.

_____ = ____

____ × ____ = ____

6.

_____ = ____

____ × ____ = ____

7.

_____ = ____

____ × ____ = ____

8.

_____ = ____

____ × ____ = ____

Array Punch

Materials: hole punch, small pieces of sturdy colored paper, glue

Directions: Look at each multiplication sentence. Choose a piece of colored paper. Use the hole punch to punch an array on the colored paper that matches the multiplication sentence at the top of the card. Then, glue the array below the multiplication sentence.

3 × 5	5 × 2
4 × 3	2 × 3
5 × 5	3 × 2
2 × 5	5 × 3

To prep: Make copies of the activity sheet and place in a center. Provide small pieces of sturdy colored paper in the station for students to use. The pieces should be small enough so that they can be glued below each problem, but large enough for students to punch holes in to create matching arrays. Cut off these directions before copying.

Reading and Writing Numbers

 ## Essential Question

How can place value be used to model and write 3-digit numbers?

Warm-Up/Review

Give each place value a sound or action. For example, a clap for hundreds, a snap for tens, and a stomp for ones. Write a 3-digit number on the board. Underline one of the digits. Have students perform the action that corresponds with the place value of the underlined digit. Repeat the activity.

 ## Mini-Lesson

Materials: base ten blocks

1. Use base ten blocks to review place value. Show how 10 units make 1 rod and 10 rods make 1 flat. Discuss the term *digit* and give examples of 1-, 2-, and 3-digit numbers.

2. Write a 3-digit number on the board. Model how to use base ten blocks to show the number. Explain that the order is always ones, tens, hundreds when moving from right to left.

3. Ask, "What is the value of each digit in this number?" Show how to use those values to write the number in expanded form. (For example, $100 + 60 + 4$)

4. Demonstrate how to model and write a 3-digit number with a 0 in the ones or tens place. Point out how the expanded form does not include the 0.

5. Say a 3-digit number aloud. Ask volunteers to build the base ten model and write the number in expanded form, standard form, and word form.

6. Say more 3-digit numbers. Have students practice building base ten models with each number. Then, they should write the number in expanded form, standard form, and word form.

 ## Math Talk

What does the word *value* mean?
How would you explain place value to a friend?
Why do you still have to include a place value when the value is 0?

 ## Journal Prompt

Why is it important to be able to read and write numbers in different forms?

Materials

base ten blocks
counters (optional)

 Workstations

Activity sheets (pages 47–49)
Place Value Four-in-a-Row
(page 50)

 Guided Math

○ **Remediation: Relating Numbers to Place Value**

1. Review the term *digit*. Ask, "How many different 1-digit numbers can you write?" Have students use base ten cubes or counters to model different 1-digit numbers. Emphasize that the digit represents the ones place.

2. Draw a place value chart with two columns. Identify them as the ones and tens places. Discuss numbers you can make with two place value spaces. Have students model 2-digit numbers with base ten blocks. Demonstrate how to write the numbers in expanded form and standard form.

3. Repeat step 2 with 3-digit numbers, identifying the hundreds place.

4. Have students use base ten blocks to build 2- and 3-digit numbers. Have them record the numbers in standard and expanded form and identify the place value for each digit.

☐ **On Level: Representing Numbers**

1. Say a 3-digit number. Ask, "What are some different ways to show this number?" Give students base ten blocks and paper and pencils to model the number in different ways.

2. Show a 3-digit number using base ten blocks. Direct students to write this number in expanded form using the model as their guide. Ask, "How is writing numbers in expanded form like showing numbers with base ten blocks? How do you show place value for each digit with each method?"

3. Show a 3-digit number with a 0 in the ones place using base ten blocks, such as 250. Ask, "How do we represent the 0 in the ones place when writing this number in expanded form?" Model how to write the expanded form of the number. Then, continue to say other 2- and 3-digit numbers. Have students write the standard and expanded forms of the numbers. Have students use base ten blocks to support their answers.

4. Have students write a number in standard form. Students should switch with a partner and draw a picture of the new number in base ten blocks and write it in expanded form.

△ **Enrichment: Exploring Place Value**

1. Model the number *2,050*. Ask, "What do you do when there is a 0 in a place value? Does it matter whether you write a 0 in the standard form? (Yes) Does it matter whether you write a 0 in the expanded form? (No) Can you write an additional 0 in either form and not change the value of the number? (Only in expanded form) How can you check to see if you have the correct expanded form?"

2. Write several 3- and 4-digit numbers on chart paper. Build an incorrect model for one of the numbers and write an incorrect expanded form for one of the numbers. (For example, for 5,724, write 4 + 500 + 2,000 + 70.) Ask, "What errors, if any, did I make? What should I change so that the models or expanded forms match the numbers? Does the order of numbers matter in expanded form? (No) Does the order of numbers matter in standard form? (Yes)"

3. Have students explain the difference between the numbers 1,509 and 1,590.

 Assess and Extend

Have students write the expanded, standard, and word form of the number *355*. Then, have them draw the number in base ten blocks. For an added challenge, have them repeat the activity with the number *1,001*.

Reading and Writing Numbers

Write each number in expanded form. The first one has been done for you.

1.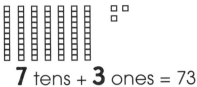

_7_ tens + **_3_** ones = 73

2.

_____ ten + _____ ones = 18

3.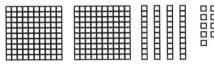

_____ hundreds + _____ tens + _____ ones = 249

4.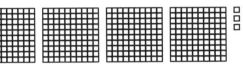

_____ hundreds + _____ tens + _____ ones = 405

5.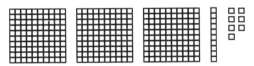

_____ hundreds + _____ ten + _____ ones = 317

Write the value of the underlined digit. The first one has been done for you.

6. 3̲8

_____**3 tens**_____ = __**30**__

7. 5̲2̲

_____ = _____

8. 2̲7̲4

_____ = _____

9. 6̲19

_____ = _____

10. 8̲01

_____ = _____

Reading and Writing Numbers   ☐ Representing Numbers

Write each number in expanded form and in standard form.

1.

_____ + _____ = _____

2.

_____ + _____ = _____

3.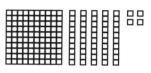

_____ + _____ + _____ = _____

4.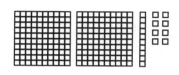

_____ + _____ + _____ = _____

5.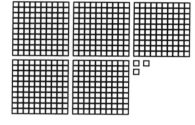

_____ + _____ = _____

6.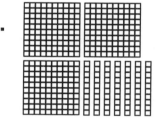

_____ + _____ = _____

Write each number in expanded form.

7. 419

_____

8. 280

_____

9. 735

_____

10. 607

_____

Write each number in standard form.

11. 900 + 30 + 5   _____

12. 400 + 8   _____

13. 300 + 10 + 2   _____

14. 800 + 60   _____

Reading and Writing Numbers ▲ Exploring Place Value

Circle the matching number for each model. Then, write the number in expanded form.

1.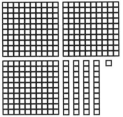
131
314
341 _____

2.
128
1,028
1,208 _____

3.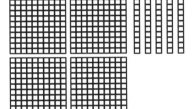
45
405
450 _____

4.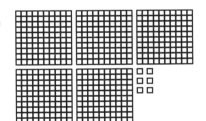
56
506
560 _____

Write each number in standard form.

5. seven hundred sixty

_____

6. three thousand sixteen

_____

7. two thousand eighty

_____

8. nine hundred one

_____

9. one thousand three hundred twelve

_____

Place Value Four-in-a-Row

Materials: 1 die, 2 game pieces, two-colored counters

To play: Place the game pieces on START. Take turns rolling the die and moving that many spaces on the outer path. Look at the number form on the space you landed on. Find the matching number on the inner board. Mark it with a counter. The first player to fill five spaces in a row wins the game. Only place a counter on a FREE space when it completes a four-in-a-row set.

three hundred thirty-three	[base-ten blocks]	[base-ten blocks]	90 + 9	600 + 50 + 2	twenty-five	500 + 90 + 6
400 + 10	57	410	612	711	FREE	[base-ten blocks]
sixty-eight	447	FREE	652	601	25	400 + 40 + 7
50 + 7	FREE	125	68	596	10	six hundred twelve
[base-ten blocks]	22	75	165	FREE	99	
START	119	217	950	333	562	600 + 1
[base-ten blocks]	seven hundred eleven	500 + 60 + 2	[base-ten blocks]	one hundred twenty-five	nine hundred fifty	

Understanding Place Value

 Essential Question

What is the value of each number in a 3-digit number?

Warm-Up/Review

Skip count by tens to 100 aloud as a class. Then, have students open and close their hands (10 fingers) in the air to skip count by tens to 100 again. Finally, have students stand and jump up in the air (10 toes) to skip count by tens to 100 one final time.

 Mini-Lesson

1. Write *ones*, *tens*, and *hundreds* on the board. Explain that the place value names help us talk about the digits and know their values.

2. Write *389* on the board. Ask "What is the place value of the digit 8? What is its value? Is it worth only 8?" Explain, "It means that there are 8 tens. Its value is 80." Demonstrate skip counting by 10 eight times until you get to 80. Then, ask "What digit in 389 has the highest value?" Explain that the digit 3 has the highest value because it is in the hundreds place and is worth 300.

3. Write the number *200* on the board. Ask, "Why are there zeros in the tens and ones places?" Explain that even though only 2 hundreds are needed to show the number, you need to write a 0 in the tens and ones places to show that there are no tens or ones in the number.

4. Continue working with other numbers, focusing on the place value names and their values.

5. Have pairs of students swap number riddles, such as "I have 2 tens, 4 hundreds, and 0 ones. What number am I?" Students should write the answers in standard form.

 Math Talk

How can tens be grouped to make 100?
How are ones and tens related?
What is the value of this digit? How do
   you know?

 Journal Prompt

Explain how to determine the value of a digit in a number.

Materials

place value index cards (see below)
number cards 0–9 (include 2 zeros in
   each set)
base ten blocks
place value mats

 Workstations

Activity sheets (pages 53–55)
Draw, Sketch, Write (page 56)
Place Value Four-in-a-Row
   (page 50)

 Guided Math

○ **Remediation: Using Manipulatives to Identify Place Value**
   1. Give each student index cards with the place value names written on them (*ones, tens, hundreds*). Also, have number cards and base ten blocks available.
   2. Have students put the index cards in the correct order in front of them. Using number cards, have them show you *267*. Now, have them place the correct number of base ten blocks under each digit. Ask, "What digit is in the hundreds place? Which place is the 7 in?"
   3. To determine the value of each number, count base ten blocks with the group. Ask, "What is the value of 2? What is the value of 6?"
   4. Have students help you write the number in expanded form. Explain as you go, "There are 2 hundreds, so the value is 200. Six tens is 60, and 7 ones is 7, so 200 + 60 + 7 = 267."
   5. Continue working with other numbers in the same manner. Then, have partners say numbers to each other. Students should show each number in base ten blocks.

□ **On Level: Expanded Form within 1,000**
   1. Give each student number cards and a place value mat.
   2. Have students show you the number 823 by arranging the number cards on the place value mat.
   3. Ask, "What digit is in the hundreds place? What is the value of the 2? What place is the 3 in?" Have students replace all of the number cards after the named digit with zeros to see its value.
   4. Display the problem *50 + 200 + 7*. Ask students to write the number in standard form. Ask, "What did you do when you noticed the numbers were not in descending order?"
   5. Continue working with other numbers. Eventually, remove the place value mats and have students work without them.

△ **Enrichment: Number Forms Including 1,000**
   1. Give students a set of number cards and have them each choose three cards at random.
   2. Have students make the smallest and then the largest number possible with the digits. Ask, "How did you make your decision to place the digits? How did you deal with zeros?"
   3. Have students continue pulling three number cards. They should rearrange the digits to make the smallest and largest numbers possible.
   4. Write *678*. Model how to write the number in expanded form. Have students pull three number cards, create a 3-digit number, and write it in expanded form. Continue practicing with other numbers.
   5. For an added challenge, ask, "If I add 1,000 to 678, what will the sum be?" Have students use mental math or a place value mat to solve the problem. Then, have them write the expanded form of the number.

 Assess and Extend

Say a mystery number. For example, "The mystery number has a 5 in the hundreds place, a 2 in the ones place, and a 7 in the tens place. What number is it?" Have students write the numerals in the correct order to create the number.

Understanding Place Value
⬤ Using Manipulatives to Identify Place Value

Count the hundreds, tens, and ones. Write the number.

1. 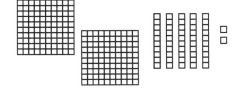 =

H	T	O

2. 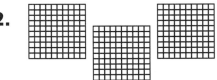 =

H	T	O

3. 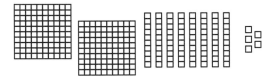 =

H	T	O

4. 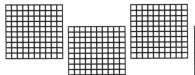 =

H	T	O

5. =

H	T	O

6. 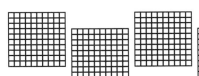 =

H	T	O

7. 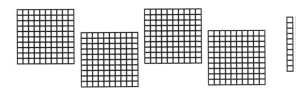 =

H	T	O

Understanding Place Value
 Expanded Form within 1,000

Draw the number using base ten blocks. Then, write the number in expanded form.

1. 402

_____ + _____ + _____

2. 523

_____ + _____ + _____

3. 630

_____ + _____ + _____

4. 241

_____ + _____ + _____

5. 87

_____ + _____

6. 472

_____ + _____ + _____

Understanding Place Value   ▲ Number Forms Including 1,000

Write the place and the value of each underlined digit.

Number	Place	Value
3<u>4</u>5	tens	40
1. 13<u>4</u>		
2. 8<u>7</u>		
3. <u>7</u>63		
4. <u>6</u>04		
5. 5<u>3</u>3		
6. <u>4</u>87		
7. <u>2</u>09		
8. 7<u>4</u>7		
9. 9<u>1</u>		
10. <u>1</u>,235		

Write the expanded form of each number.

11. 971 _____

12. 145 _____

13. 86 _____

14. 230 _____

15. 952 _____

Draw, Sketch, Write

Materials: playing cards (or several sets of 0–9 number cards)

To play: Draw a card. Write the number drawn in the place value chart in the hundreds place box (aces equal 1, face cards equal 0). Draw again and write the number in the tens place box. Draw one more time and write the number in the ones place box. Use base ten blocks to draw the number. Finally, write the number in expanded form.

Draw	Sketch	Write
H T O		
H T O		
H T O		
H T O		
H T O		
H T O		

Skip Counting

 Essential Question

How can skip counting by 5s, 10s, and 100s help with counting to 1,000?

 Warm-Up/Review

Have students count aloud the number of shoes in the class by 2s. Students should do the same with toes, with each student counting the toes on each foot by 5s. Finally, have students count the number of fingers in the class, with each student counting all of her fingers by 10s.

⭐ **Mini-Lesson**

Materials: hundred charts, two-color counters

1. Review the term *skip counting*. Give each student a hundred chart and counters. Look at the hundred chart together. Start at 5 and skip count to 100, placing counters as you count aloud. Ask, "What do you notice about these numbers?" Point out that multiples of 5 always have a 0 or a 5 in the ones place.

2. Remove the counters. Start at 10 and skip count to 100, placing different color counters as you count aloud. Point out that multiples of 10 always have a 0 in the ones place. Challenge students to continue skip counting aloud to 200 by 10s.

3. Using the hundred chart, point to a multiple of 5 and model how to skip count forward and backward from this number. Repeat with a multiple of 10.

4. Finally, as a class, count aloud to 1,000 by 100s.

5. Have pairs of students practice skip counting by 5s and 10s from a given number.

 Math Talk

What patterns can you see in a hundred chart?
Explain skip counting.
Can you skip count by 3s? 4s?

 Journal Prompt

What is skip counting useful for? When have you used skip counting in real life?

Materials

copies of a 120 chart
blank number lines
nickel and dime manipulatives
graph paper

 Workstations

Activity sheets (pages 59–61)
Spin-a-Skip (page 62)

 Guided Math

⚪ **Remediation: Practicing Skip Counting**

1. Ask, "How many fingers are on each hand? How many toes are on each foot? How could I find the total number of fingers or toes here in the group? What is a quick way to find that sum?" Skip count the total number of fingers together. Repeat with the total number of toes.

2. Give each student a 120 chart. Review the pattern of digits in the ones place for multiples of 5. Have students color all of the multiples of 5 on a 120 chart. Ask, "What digits do each of these numbers end in? Does this make it easier to spot them on the chart?" Then, review the pattern of digits in the ones place for multiples of 10.

3. Start from different multiples of 5 and 10 and model how to skip count forward and backward from each number. Practice this several times as a group, then in student pairs.

4. Say a number aloud. Have students skip count (by 5s or 10s) and write the next five numbers. Repeat with other numbers.

◻ **On Level: Using Skip Counting**

1. Discuss the benefit of skip counting versus counting each unit of a large set.

2. Use a number line beginning at 425 to count to 500 by 5s, drawing an arched line to "hop" to each multiple of 5. Then, count backward by 5s on the number line to 425, starting at 500.

3. Use a number line beginning at 210 to count to 320 by tens, drawing an arched line to "hop" to each multiple of 10.

4. Gather a large pile of nickels. Ask, "How much is each nickel worth? How can you count the total amount of money you have?" Explain that they can skip count the pile of nickels by 5s to know how much money is there. Skip count the money together. Repeat with a large handful of dimes. Skip count the pile of dimes by 10s as a class to get the total amount.

5. Have partners repeat the activity with random handfuls of nickels and dimes.

△ **Enrichment: Relating Skip Counting to Multiplication**

1. Skip count aloud by 5s beginning at 50 and ending at 105. List the numbers as you say them. Explain that these numbers are called *multiples of 5*. Ask, "What numbers do multiples of 5 end in? Are multiples of 5 even or odd numbers?" Discuss how some multiples of 5 are even and some are odd. Repeat the activity with multiples of 10. Note that multiples of 10 are always even.

2. Distribute graph paper to students. Have them color squares to make 4 rows of 5. Ask, "How can you write the number of rows of 5 as an addition sentence? As a multiplication sentence?" Model skip counting by 5s as you point to each row. Point out how many rows you counted and write the related multiplication sentence. Ask, "How many rows of 5 would you need to color 45 squares?" (9) Continue with other factors of 5.

3. Have students discuss how skip counting is related to multiplication.

 Assess and Extend

Write a word problem on the board that can be solved by skip counting, such as *There are 10 hot dogs in a package. How many hot dogs are in 7 packages?* Have students solve the problem and explain how they used skip counting to find the answer.

Name _____   Date _____

Skip Counting

Skip count to find the total number in each group.

I.

_____ triangles

2.

_____ circles

3.

_____ stars

Skip count by 5s or 10s. Write the missing numbers in each list.

4. 25, 30, _____, 40, 45, _____, 55, 60

5. _____, 70, 80, _____, _____, 110

6. 50, 55, _____, _____, _____, 75, _____

7. _____, 140, 145, 150, _____, _____, _____, 170

8. _____, 20, _____, 40, _____, _____, 70, _____

Skip Counting

Skip count by 5s.

1.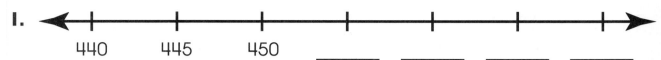
440   445   450   ____   ____   ____   ____

2.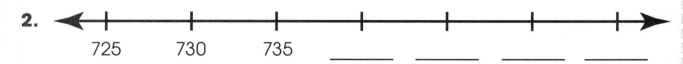
725   730   735   ____   ____   ____   ____

3. 245, 250, 255, 260, _____, _____, _____, _____

4. 310, 315, 320, 325, _____, _____, _____, _____

Skip count by 10s.

5.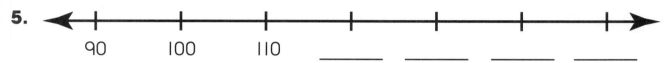
90   100   110   ____   ____   ____   ____

6.
415   425   435   ____   ____   ____   ____

7. 910, 920, 930, 940, _____, _____, _____, _____

8. 635, 645, 655, 665, _____, _____, _____, _____

Skip count by 100s.

9.
____   230   330   430   ____   ____   ____

10.
290   390   490   ____   ____   ____   ____

11. 195, 295, 395, 495, _____, _____, _____, _____

12. 224, 324, 424, 524, _____, _____, _____, _____

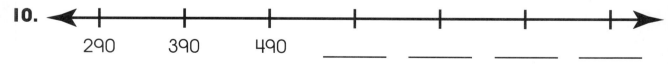

Skip Counting ▲ Relating Skip Counting to Multiplication

Write a multiplication problem for each array.

1. ☐☐☐☐☐
☐☐☐☐☐

_____ × _____ = _____

2.

_____ × _____ = _____

3. ☐☐☐☐☐
☐☐☐☐☐
☐☐☐☐☐
☐☐☐☐☐
☐☐☐☐☐
☐☐☐☐☐

_____ × _____ = _____

4. ☐☐☐☐☐
☐☐☐☐☐
☐☐☐☐☐
☐☐☐☐☐
☐☐☐☐☐

_____ × _____ = _____

Use skip counting to answer each question. Draw a picture to show each problem.

5. A watermelon is cut into 6 slices. Each slice has 5 seeds in it. How many total seeds are in the watermelon?

6. A chef bakes 5 pizzas. Each pizza is cut into 10 equal slices. How many total slices of pizza did the chef bake?

Spin-a-Skip

Materials: sharpened pencil, paper clip

To play: For each round, two players take turns spinning the spinner using the sharpened pencil and paper clip. If the spinner lands on *5s*, begin at the last number written and skip count by 5s to the next number. Write that number in the next box. If the spinner lands on *10s*, skip count by 10s from the last number written and write it in the next box. If the spinner lands on *100s*, skip count to 100 from the previous number and record it. Continue playing until each player's board is filled. The player with the highest ending number wins the round.

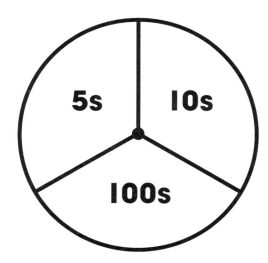

Round 1

Player 1	10				
Player 2	10				

Round 2

Player 1	30				
Player 2	30				

Round 3

Player 1	50				
Player 2	50				

Comparing Numbers

 Essential Question

How can place value and symbols be used to compare numbers?

Warm-Up/Review

Write the numbers *36, 50, 78, 16, 10, 22,* and *62* on the board. Have a volunteer circle the numbers that are greater than 50 in one color. Have another volunteer circle the numbers that are less than 50 with a different color. Finally, have a volunteer circle the number that is equal to 50.

 Mini-Lesson

Materials: base ten blocks

1. Use base ten blocks to compare two numbers. Model *30* and *50.* Remind students that each rod is made of 10 units. Write the standard form of each number under the models.

2. Emphasize that when comparing numbers, start with the largest place value to compare. Ask, "What digit is in the tens place in the first number? What digit is in the tens place in the second number? Which model has more rods? Which number is greater?"

3. Have students build models for the numbers *42* and *46.* Start with the largest place value of the two numbers. The two numbers have an equal amount in the tens place. Compare the ones place. Ask, "Which number has more units in the ones place?" Say, "46 is greater than 42, and 42 is less than 46" to reinforce the relationship. Review the symbols for *less than* (<), *greater than* (>), and *equal to* (=).

4. Practice comparing several more pairs of 2-digit numbers. Include pairs with equal tens places. Ask students to identify the greater number in each pair.

5. Repeat steps 3 and 4 with 3-digit numbers. Include pairs with equal hundreds and tens places.

 Math Talk

What are some things that might happen if numbers were not ordered?
What does the word *equal* mean?
When would you want to compare numbers?

 Journal Prompt

Explain how you know if a number is greater than, less than, or equal to another number.

Materials

base ten blocks

 Workstations

Activity sheets (pages 65–67)
Compare-a-Spin (page 68)

 Guided Math

◯ **Remediation: Reinforcing Comparative Sentences**

1. Write the numbers *45* and *36* on the board. Ask, "What does each digit stand for in these numbers?" Have students build each number using base ten blocks.

2. Looking at the models, ask, "Which number has more tens rods? Which has more ones units? Which place value tells which number is greater? Which number is greater?" Reinforce the relationship with comparative sentences. (For example, *36 is less than 45*, or *45 is greater than 36*.)

3. Use the same process to compare additional pairs of 2-digit numbers. Remind students to always start with the largest place value. Identify the digit in each place and use math vocabulary to compare the numbers. Allow students who are ready to move on to 3-digit numbers.

4. Have students describe the process of comparing numbers with a partner.

▢ **On Level: Comparing Numbers**

1. Review place value and reinforce that place value increases from right to left. Write the numbers *28* and *37* on the board. Ask, "What digits are in the ones and tens places of each number? Which place value do we compare first? Which number is greater?" Build each model with base ten blocks to confirm. Compare the numbers using the appropriate greater than and less than symbols.

2. Follow the same process with the numbers *156* and *162*. Ask, "What is the largest place value in these numbers? Can you use this place value to tell which number is greater? How can you compare these numbers?" Show students how to move to the next largest place value in each number and compare.

3. Explain how to compare two numbers with different place values, such as *19* and *134*. Ask, "How can you quickly tell which number is greater?"

4. Have students write pairs of numbers and switch with partners to compare them using the symbols <, >, and =.

△ **Enrichment: Ordering Numbers**

1. Write *270*, *217*, and *372* on the board. Ask, "What is the name of the largest place value in each of these three numbers? Can you compare these numbers using only the hundreds place?"

2. Compare 372 to 270 and 217. Ask, "Which is the greatest number in this set? How can you tell?"

3. Next, look at 270 and 217. Ask, "Can you tell which number is greater from the hundreds place only? How can you compare them?" Model how to use the tens place to compare the digits in the first two numbers.

4. Order the numbers using symbols. (217 < 270 < 372; or 372 > 270 > 217) Ask students to read the comparison aloud.

5. Have students discuss how to compare 846, 748, and 864.

 Assess and Extend

Write *145* and *231* on the board. Have students use the symbols <, >, or = to compare them. Then, repeat with the numbers *437* and *445*. Finally, write *767* and *767* on the board and have students use the correct symbol to compare the numbers.

Comparing Numbers   Reinforcing Comparative Sentences

Write the number shown by each model. Then, circle the greater number in each pair. The first one has been done for you.

1.

   ___29___   (31)

2.

   _____   _____

3.

   _____   _____

4.

   _____   _____

5.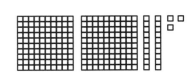

   _____   _____

Write the numbers on the correct lines to make each statement true.

6. 50   68   _____ is greater than _____.

7. 27   21   _____ is less than _____.

8. 43   34   _____ is less than _____.

Name _____ **Date** _____

Comparing Numbers   ■ Comparing Numbers

Write the number shown by each model. Then, circle the number that is greater than that number.

1.   _____   62   63   65

2. 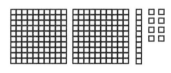   _____   29   210   223

3. 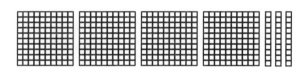   _____   45   403   435

Write > or < to make the sentence true.

4. 39 ◯ 24   **5.** 167 ◯ 169

6. 280 ◯ 208   **7.** 917 ◯ 97

8. 426 ◯ 430   **9.** 753 ◯ 751

Use > or < to write a true comparison statement for each pair of numbers.

10. 615, 561 _____

11. 380, 308 _____

12. 472, 427 _____

66   © Carson-Dellosa • CD-104954

Comparing Numbers   ▲ Ordering Numbers

Write each set of numbers in order from least to greatest.

1. 85, 58, 95 _____

2. 32, 25, 53 _____

3. 174, 157, 147 _____

4. 304, 430, 340 _____

5. 591, 590, 509 _____

6. 76, 761, 716 _____

7. 483, 487, 49 _____

Write >, <, or = to make each sentence true.

8. 342 ◯ 391   **9.** 217 ◯ 207

10. 1,060 ◯ 1,060   **11.** 538 ◯ 835

12. 900 ◯ 897   **13.** 568 ◯ 658

14. 247 ◯ 242 ◯ 238   **15.** 672 ◯ 492 ◯ 492

Compare-a-Spin

Materials: sharpened pencil, paper clip, dry-erase markers

To play: First, have each player write different 2- and 3-digit numbers in the blank spaces on his card. For each round, two players take turns spinning the spinner using a sharpened pencil and paper clip. After each spin, the player must use the symbol he landed on to make a true comparison on his card. If the player cannot make a true comparison, he loses his turn. The first player to complete his card wins the round.

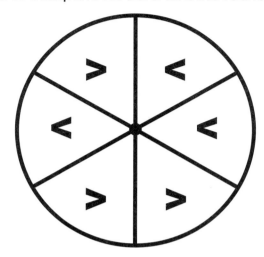

Player 1 _____

Player 2 _____

To prep: Copy on card stock and laminate for durability and so it can be used with dry-erase markers. Cut off these directions before copying and laminating.

Addition Strategies

 Essential Question

What strategies can be used to add 2-digit numbers?

Warm-Up/Review

Play a game of Around the World with addition flash cards to review basic math facts.

 Mini-Lesson

Materials: number line

1. Practice counting from 0 to 15 by calling students to the front of the classroom. Have students count aloud with you as you start with no one (0) up front. Count as you call up 1 student, then another (2), and another (3), until you reach 15 students. Allow students to return to their seats.

2. Call 11 students to the front of the room. Ask students to count how many classmates are standing up front. Next, call 7 more students to the front of the room. Ask, "How many students are up front now? What was your strategy for finding the answer?" Some may count from 1 to 18, others may start with 11 and count on, and others may use known math facts to add 11 + 7.

3. Demonstrate each of these strategies and model each one on a number line as you count the students again together.

4. Write two simple addition number sentences on the board. Have partners solve the problems and discuss which strategy they used to find the answer.

 Math Talk

What addition strategies do you use? Why?
Why is it easier to count on from a given number?
How does knowing your basic math facts help you to add larger numbers?

 Journal Prompt

Explain how to add on a number line. Provide an example.

Materials

counters
number lines
1–3 number cubes
dice
ten frames

 Workstations

Activity sheets (pages 71–73)
Math Robots (page 74)

 Guided Math

⚪ **Remediation: Comparing Methods**

1. Ask students to model *16 + 4* using counters. Have them count 16 counters in one group and 4 counters in another group, then add by counting the total by 1s to 20.

2. Show students how to use a number line to count on, sharing that it is faster than starting from 0. Ask students to model *16 + 4* using number lines. Have each student place a counter at 16 on the number line, then add by moving the counter along the number line 4 times to 20 while counting aloud.

3. Allow students to practice using both methods with a variety of facts. Ask, "What is the difference between adding using a number line and adding using counters? Which do you prefer? Why?"

⬜ **On Level: Counting On and the Commutative Property**

1. Have each student roll two number cubes and mark that number with a counter on a number line (using the first number rolled for the tens place, and the other number rolled for the ones place). Direct students to roll one die and count on to add that many more to the marked number. They may point to each number as they count on or move the counter to each number to find the answer.

2. Ask students to write the problem as a number sentence. Then, have them write the same problem with the addends in a different order and model the new equation on their number lines. Ask, "Is the answer still the same? Which number is easier to start with? Why?"

3. Allow students to practice adding different facts and writing the related fact for each one using the commutative property.

△ **Enrichment: Mentally Adding By Making 10s**

1. Say, "When we add two numbers, we can look for a way to make a ten." Write the equation *18 + 9 =*. Model the equation on 3 ten frames by decomposing 18 into 10 and 8. Model your thinking aloud. Point out the 8 counters on the second ten frame. Ask, "What can I add to this ten frame to make a ten?" Move two counters from the third ten frame (with 9 counters) onto the second ten frame to make another 10, leaving 7 counters on the last ten frame.

2. Say, "Now, look at our ten frames. What number is now composed on the frames?" (27) Say, "We can count the ten frames: 10 plus 10 plus 7 equals 27."

3. Explain, "Another way to solve it is by using known facts. Since we know that 8 + 9 = 17, we can mentally add the 10 (from 18), which makes 27." Practice the strategies as a group with several more addition problems.

4. Present students with an addition problem such as *37 + 9 = ___*. Instruct students to use the ten frames to add these numbers using the "make a ten" strategy and write the sum.

5. Have students explain how they know their answers are correct.

 Assess and Extend

Write *28 + 4 =* and *43 + 8 =* on the board. (32, 51) Students should solve the problems and explain which strategy they used to solve each one.

Addition Strategies   ● Comparing Methods

Add to find the total number of objects. Write the sum.

1. 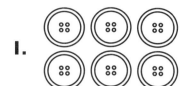 + (buttons) = _____

2. (dots) + (dots) = _____

3. (stars) + (stars) = _____

4. (boxes) + (boxes) = _____

Count on the number line to add. The starting point is marked for you. Circle your answer.

5. 15 + 3

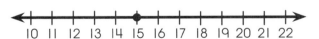

6. 17 + 4

7. 12 + 8

8. 10 + 7

9. 16 + 6

10. 22 + 0

71

Name _____   Date _____

Addition Strategies

Roll a number cube once for each number line. Count on to add that amount. The starting point is marked for you. Circle your answer. Then, write the same problem in another way.

1. 18 + _____ = _____

_____ + _____ = _____

2. 29 + _____ = _____

_____ + _____ = _____

3. 22 + _____ = _____

_____ + _____ = _____

4. 16 + _____ = _____

_____ + _____ = _____

5. 11 + _____ = _____

_____ + _____ = _____

6. 31 + _____ = _____

_____ + _____ = _____

7. 20 + _____ = _____

_____ + _____ = _____

8. 44 + _____ = _____

_____ + _____ = _____

Addition Strategies ▲ Mentally Adding by Making 10s

Solve. Show your thinking with words, numbers, or pictures.

I. 28 + 18 = _____

2. 35 + 16 = _____

3. 47 + 15 = _____

4. 29 + 61 = _____

5. 44 + 38 = _____

6. 22 + 38 = _____

Math Robots

Materials: scrap paper

To play: For each turn, players should think of two numbers that would fill in the blanks to make a correct addition sentence. Player 1 should write his equation on a scrap of paper and place it facedown to the side. Player 2 should guess a single digit to fill in one of the blanks. Cross off the digit from the list. If she guesses correctly, Player 1 fills it in on the equation. If the digit is not in the equation, trace a part of the math robot's face. Player 2 continues guessing numbers until the entire equation is complete or until the math robot's face is completely filled in. If all seven sections get filled in, the player guessing loses. Reveal the equation if the player guessing correctly fills in the blanks.

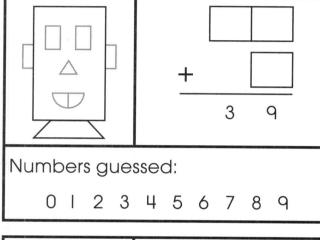

Numbers guessed:

0 1 2 3 4 5 6 7 8 9

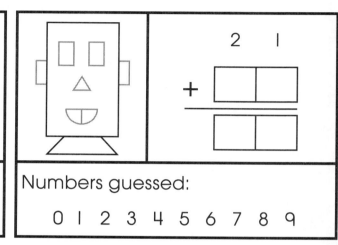

Numbers guessed:

0 1 2 3 4 5 6 7 8 9

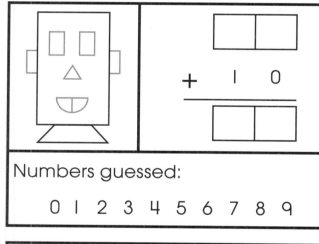

Numbers guessed:

0 1 2 3 4 5 6 7 8 9

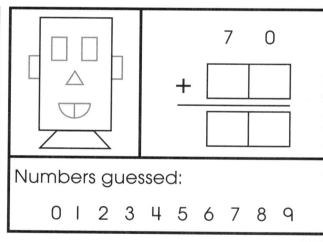

Numbers guessed:

0 1 2 3 4 5 6 7 8 9

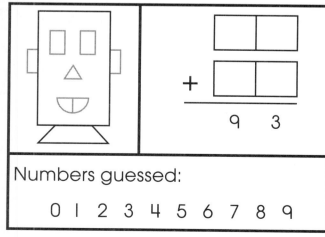

Numbers guessed:

0 1 2 3 4 5 6 7 8 9

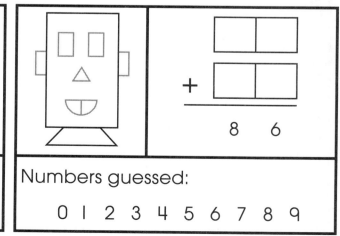

Numbers guessed:

0 1 2 3 4 5 6 7 8 9

Addition with Regrouping

Essential Question

How is place value used when adding with regrouping?

Warm-Up/Review

Write several addition problems on the board that do not require regrouping. Have students solve the problems.

 ## Mini-Lesson

Materials: base ten blocks

1. Draw a place value chart showing ones and tens. Write *45 + 29* vertically in the chart. Explain, "When we add, it is important to line up digits correctly—ones with ones and tens with tens."

2. Say, "When I add 5 + 9, it equals 14, but there is only room for 1 digit." If desired, demonstrate writing *14* in the ones place and continuing to solve the problem to find a sum of 614. Discuss how the answer is too large to be the correct sum. Then, model the concept of carrying with the base ten blocks. Put 9 cubes and 5 cubes together. Then, count the total (14). Say, "I can trade 10 cubes for a tens rod and still have 14." Count the blocks to confirm. "I write the 4 in the ones column because there are 4 ones cubes. Then, I carry the tens rod over to the tens column." Record a *1* above the tens place.

3. Point to the tens column. "I have 4 tens, 2 tens, and 1 ten for a total of 7 tens." Write *7* in the tens column.

4. Repeat steps 1–3 with other equations that require regrouping.

5. Write other equations for students to solve with partners. Students should explain to their partner how to regroup.

 ## Math Talk

Why do we need to align digits in the proper place value column when adding?
What happens when you do not align ones with ones, tens with tens, etc.?
Explain regrouping to a friend.

 ## Journal Prompt

Explain why this problem is wrong: *39 + 93 = 1,212*. How do you know it is wrong? Solve the problem correctly.

Materials

base ten blocks
laminated place value mats
dry-erase markers

 Workstations

Activity sheets (pages 77–79)
Spin-to-Add (page 80)
Math Robots (page 74)

 Guided Math

○ **Remediation: Reinforcing the Process**

1. Write *43 + 15*. Have students build each number using base ten blocks, stacking the two models and aligning place values on a place value mat.
2. Ask, "Where do we begin adding? Where do we write the sum?" Count the ones units together and write 8 in the ones column. Then, count the total number of rods and write it in the tens column. Read the sum and confirm that the base ten blocks show 58.
3. Write *64 + 29*. Ask, "What is the sum of the ones place? What do you do when the sum of a column is greater than 9?" Model how to exchange 10 units for 1 rod. Explain that this is called regrouping. Let students practice regrouping ones into tens with random handfuls of ones units.
4. Write addition problems with and without regrouping. Have students find the sums using base ten blocks to support their solutions.

☐ **On Level: Hands-On Adding**

1. Write *39 + 44* and show students how to line up the problem by ones and tens using base ten blocks on a place value mat. As you place base ten blocks, say, "The first number is 39, which has 3 tens and 9 ones; the second number has 4 tens and 4 ones." Have students count the blocks along with you.
2. Say, "First, I add the ones column, 9 plus 4." Pull all of the cubes together and count them. "Because I can't put the number 13 in the ones column, I trade 10 cubes for a tens rod. Now, I have 3 cubes left and 1 tens rod. I write 3 in the ones column. Then, I carry the tens rod to the tens column."
3. As you add the tens, explain, "3 tens plus 4 tens plus 1 ten equals 8 tens." Have students count their own blocks with you and write the results in the appropriate columns. Ask students to read their sums. Read the entire equation, pointing to each addend and the sum on the board.
4. Continue practicing with equations that require regrouping. Have students practice without base ten blocks when ready.

△ **Enrichment: Regrouping More Than Once**

1. Write *644 + 269*. Model solving the problem, asking students to talk you through it as you work. Ask, "What column do I add first? 4 plus 9 equals 13. Can I put a 2-digit number in the ones column? Which digit do I write in the ones column and which goes in the tens column?"
2. Continue, "In the tens place, I add 4 tens plus 6 tens plus 1 ten. That equals 11 tens. Can I put a 2-digit number in the tens column?" Lead students to understand that you have to regroup again. Walk through solving the rest of the problem. (913)
3. Continue with other problems that require regrouping more than once. Have students try the problems on their own and check their work together.

 Assess and Extend

Write *43 + 48 =* and *67 + 15 =* on the board. Have students solve the problems. (91, 82) Then, have students choose one of the problems and explain the steps they took to solve it.

Addition with Regrouping   ● Reinforcing the Process

Find each sum. Cross off the answer in the bank below.

Answer Bank

52	55	58	79	83
88	90	95	121	165

1. $\begin{array}{r} 51 \\ +\ 28 \\ \hline \end{array}$

2. $\begin{array}{r} 64 \\ +\ 24 \\ \hline \end{array}$

3. $\begin{array}{r} 37 \\ +\ 18 \\ \hline \end{array}$

4. $\begin{array}{r} 35 \\ +\ 17 \\ \hline \end{array}$

5. $\begin{array}{r} 52 \\ +\ 43 \\ \hline \end{array}$

6. $\begin{array}{r} 48 \\ +\ 42 \\ \hline \end{array}$

7. $\begin{array}{r} 37 \\ +\ 21 \\ \hline \end{array}$

8. $\begin{array}{r} 55 \\ +\ 28 \\ \hline \end{array}$

9. $\begin{array}{r} 95 \\ +\ 26 \\ \hline \end{array}$

10. $\begin{array}{r} 89 \\ +\ 76 \\ \hline \end{array}$

Addition with Regrouping

Solve each problem. Show your work.

1. $\begin{array}{r} 67 \\ +23 \\ \hline \end{array}$
  2. $\begin{array}{r} 76 \\ +5 \\ \hline \end{array}$
  3. $\begin{array}{r} 57 \\ +16 \\ \hline \end{array}$
  4. $\begin{array}{r} 35 \\ +25 \\ \hline \end{array}$
  5. $\begin{array}{r} 64 \\ +18 \\ \hline \end{array}$

6. $\begin{array}{r} 48 \\ +22 \\ \hline \end{array}$
  7. $\begin{array}{r} 45 \\ +30 \\ \hline \end{array}$
  8. $\begin{array}{r} 58 \\ +19 \\ \hline \end{array}$
  9. $\begin{array}{r} 43 \\ +14 \\ \hline \end{array}$
  10. $\begin{array}{r} 79 \\ +4 \\ \hline \end{array}$

11. $\begin{array}{r} 45 \\ +29 \\ \hline \end{array}$
  12. $\begin{array}{r} 67 \\ +13 \\ \hline \end{array}$
  13. $\begin{array}{r} 16 \\ +79 \\ \hline \end{array}$
  14. $\begin{array}{r} 98 \\ +3 \\ \hline \end{array}$
  15. $\begin{array}{r} 73 \\ +17 \\ \hline \end{array}$

16. $\begin{array}{r} 75 \\ +10 \\ \hline \end{array}$
  17. $\begin{array}{r} 28 \\ +19 \\ \hline \end{array}$
  18. $\begin{array}{r} 64 \\ +17 \\ \hline \end{array}$
  19. $\begin{array}{r} 38 \\ +29 \\ \hline \end{array}$
  20. $\begin{array}{r} 21 \\ +19 \\ \hline \end{array}$

Addition with Regrouping ▲ Regrouping More Than Once

Solve each problem. Show your work.

1.
```
  362
+ 199
```

2.
```
  414
+ 397
```

3.
```
  655
+ 298
```

4.
```
  515
+ 225
```

5.
```
  198
+  44
```

6.
```
  609
+  91
```

7.
```
  724
+  91
```

8.
```
  457
+ 111
```

9.
```
  672
+ 148
```

10.
```
  484
+ 348
```

11.
```
  453
+ 459
```

12.
```
  419
+ 192
```

13.
```
  498
+ 189
```

14.
```
  853
+ 167
```

15.
```
  444
+ 166
```

16.
```
  473
+ 448
```

17.
```
  527
+ 297
```

18.
```
  419
+ 254
```

19.
```
  289
+ 243
```

20.
```
  342
+ 199
```

Spin-to-Add

Materials: sharpened pencil, paper clip

To play: Use a sharpened pencil and a paper clip to spin the first spinner. Write the number in the top boxes. Spin the second spinner and write the number in the middle boxes. Add the two numbers together and record the total in the bottom box. Don't forget to regroup!

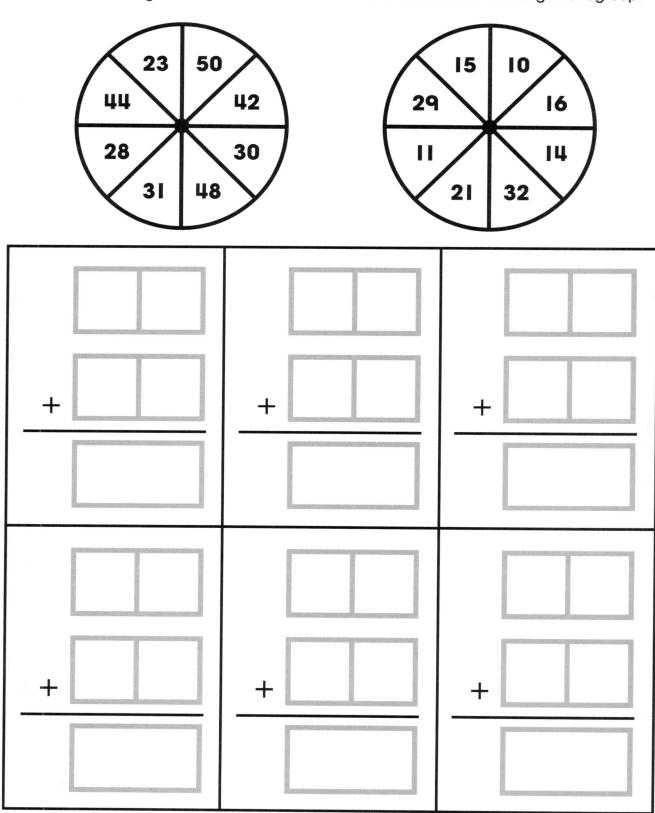

Adding Multiple 2-Digit Numbers

 Essential Question

What strategies can be used when adding multiple 2-digit numbers?

Warm-Up/Review

Write several 2-digit addition problems on the board—both with and without regrouping. Set a timer. Challenge students to see how many problems they can solve in the allotted time.

 Mini-Lesson

1. Write *87, 45,* and *62* horizontally on the board. Ask, "How can I add all three of these numbers at the same time?"

2. Have students copy the problem and align it vertically by place value.

3. Ask students to find two digits that add up to ten in the ones column. If there is not one, have them look for a familiar math fact. Remind students that when you are adding, it does not matter which way the numbers are grouped (associative property), or which order they are added in (commutative property). Say, "I do not see two digits that add up to ten in the ones column, but I do know that 5 + 2 = 7, and then my doubles facts tell me that 7 + 7 = 14." Model writing the *4* in the ones column and carrying the *1* to the top of the tens column. Review the process of regrouping. Remind students to record any regrouped number in the next column so that the value is not lost.

4. Solve the problem by adding the numbers in the tens column in the same manner, pointing out that there are two digits that add up to 10. Model aligning the 19 in the correct place value columns to complete the problem. Point out that 19 tens can be regrouped into 1 hundred and 9 tens. So, the 1 is in the hundreds place.

5. Model more problems with regrouping. Then, write *33 + 65 + 11* on the board. Have students solve the problem with partners and explain the steps they took to solve it.

 Math Talk

How does looking for a ten first help you add more easily?

What other strategies can be used to add 3- or 4-digit numbers?

When might you have to add more than two 2-digit numbers in real life?

 Journal Prompt

Explain why you can decompose numbers when adding and still get the same sum.

Materials

copies of a word problem (see below)
highlighters
base ten blocks
number line

 Workstations

Activity sheets (pages 83–85)
Domino Addition (page 86)
Spin-to-Add (page 80)

 Guided Math

⊙ **Remediation: Using Base Ten Blocks**

1. Display the following problem: *Kate read 19 pages in her book over the weekend, 13 pages on Tuesday, and 17 pages on Thursday. How many pages did she read this week?* Read the problem together. Provide a copy to each student.

2. Have students highlight the three numbers used in the problem. Work together to reframe the question as a statement to figue out what you are solving for. (Kate read ___ pages this week.) Look at the context and key words to find the operation needed to solve. Then, model how to align the three 2-digit numbers vertically.

3. Distribute base ten blocks to students. Have students model each number using base ten blocks. Demonstrate moving all of the tens rods together and all of the ones blocks together.

4. Have students regroup the ones blocks and trade out for tens rods.

5. Count the total number of tens and ones together to solve the problem. (49 pages)

6. Continue practicing adding three and four 2-digit numbers using the above strategy.

▧ **On Level: Addition Strategies**

1. Write the following: *Will solved 16 + 36 + 21 like this:*

$$10 + 30 + 20 = 60$$
$$6 + 6 + 1 = 13$$
$$60 + 13 = 73$$

2. Have a volunteer explain how Will decomposed the problem and then added. Have partners discuss why this is a good strategy.

3. Ask, "How could we also solve this problem using a number line?" Model keeping one number whole and adding the other numbers as decomposed tens and ones using a number line as a tool. (For example, 36 + 20 + 10 + 1 + 6)

4. When students are ready, introduce and practice adding four 2-digit numbers using the above strategy.

△ **Enrichment: Multiple-Digit Addition**

1. Write *9, 84,* and *567.* Ask, "How can I add three numbers with different numbers of digits? Can I align the numbers by the first digit in each number? Why must I always align numbers by the ones place?" Have students align the problem correctly and solve. (660)

2. Write examples on the board, making a different mistake (improper alignment, not regrouping, etc.) in each addition problem. Challenge students to find and correct the errors.

3. Have students discuss how to add four 2-digit numbers.

 Assess and Extend

Write the following number sentence on the board: *34 + 36 + 12 + 15 = ?*
Have students solve the problem and explain the strategy they used.

Name _____ **Date** _____

Adding Multiple 2-Digit Numbers Using Base Ten Blocks

Solve each problem. Draw base ten blocks to show your work.

I.
```
   27
   25
+  20
```

2.
```
   33
   12
+  28
```

3.
```
   29
   20
+  33
```

4.
```
   18
   31
+  22
```

5.
```
   21
   53
+  13
```

6.
```
   27
   42
+  23
```

Adding Multiple 2-Digit Numbers

Solve each problem. Show your work using expanded notation.

1.
```
    17
    16
    23
  + 18
```

2.
```
    12
    25
    26
  + 25
```

3.
```
    31
    11
    29
  + 42
```

4.
```
    29
    51
    53
  + 20
```

5.
```
    25
    24
    35
  + 36
```

6.
```
    12
    22
    47
  + 38
```

Adding Multiple 2-Digit Numbers   ▲ Multiple-Digit Addition

Solve each problem. Show your work.

1.
```
   102
   155
 + 124
```

2.
```
  1,051
    113
 +  371
```

3.
```
  1,392
    375
 +  313
```

4.
```
   437
   277
 + 222
```

5.
```
   325
   336
 + 132
```

6.
```
  2,101
    482
 +  211
```

7.
```
   233
   278
 + 193
```

8.
```
  2,765
    266
 +  199
```

9.
```
   677
   102
 +  15
```

Domino Addition

Materials: dominoes, paper bag

To play: Draw three dominoes from the bag. Record each domino as a 2-digit number to make a 2-digit addition problem with multiple addends. For example, a domino with 2 dots and 3 dots can be 23 or 32. Solve.

1.

2.

3.

4.

5.

6.

Subtraction Strategies

 Essential Question

What strategies can be used to subtract 2-digit numbers?

Warm-Up/Review

Play a game of Around the World with subtraction flash cards to review basic math facts.

 Mini-Lesson

Materials: laminated blank number lines, dry-erase markers

1. Draw a number line on the board with a starting point at 35 and an ending point at 45. Write *42 – 4* on the board.

2. Explain, "You can use different strategies to subtract. One strategy is to use a number line. You can count back 'hops' on a number line." Have students look at the problem. Circle the first number in the number sentence on the number line. Say, "You can draw 4 hops to count back 4 from 42." Demonstrate how to draw curved lines from 42 to 41, to 40, to 39, and then to 38. Encourage students to count aloud as they draw the hops. (1, 2, 3, 4)

3. Give each student a number line. Have students repeat the process with other subtraction problems. Observe as students draw the jumps and count back aloud.

4. Discuss other subtraction strategies, such as using doubles facts, using a hundred board, and recognizing fact families. Demonstrate each as time allows.

 Math Talk

Tell how you can use an addition fact to help you subtract.
Discuss how you can use place value to help you subtract.
What is the strategy you feel most comfortable using? Why?

 Journal Prompt

Explain how to use a number line to subtract. Provide an example.

Materials

hundred chart
number lines
dice
counters
base ten blocks

 Workstations

Activity sheets (pages 89–91)
Flower Power (page 92)

 Guided Math

⬤ **Remediation: Comparing Methods**

1. Ask students to model 19 – 8 using a hundred chart. Have them place their finger on 19 and move back 8 spaces. Ask, "What number did you land on?" Have students write a number sentence to match.
2. Show students how to use a number line to count back. Ask students to model 19 – 8 using number lines. Have each student place a counter at 19 on the number line, then subtract by moving the counter backward along the number line 8 times to 11.
3. Allow students to practice using both methods with a variety of facts.
4. Ask, "What is the difference between subtracting using a hundred chart and subtracting using a number line? Which do you prefer? Why?"

▢ **On Level: Subtraction and the Inverse Operation**

1. Have each student roll two dice and mark that number (using the first number rolled for the tens place, and the second number rolled for the ones place) with a counter on a number line. Then, direct students to roll one die and subtract that number using the number line. They may point to each number as they count back or move the counter to each number to find the answer.
2. Then, have students add the answer they landed on to the number they subtracted. Explain, "If the sum equals the number you subtracted from, your answer is correct." Explain that addition is the opposite of subtraction, so they are *inverse operations*.
3. Allow students to practice with a variety of facts, using the inverse operation to check their answers.

▲ **Enrichment: Expanded Form Subtraction**

1. Write *467 – 356 =* on the board. Say, "We are going to take what we know about place value and how to break numbers apart into expanded form to solve this 3-digit subtraction problem."
2. Have a volunteer demonstrate how to model the number 467 using base ten blocks. Then, have students write the expanded form. (400 + 60 + 7)
3. Ask a volunteer to represent the second number with base ten blocks. Again, have students write the second addend in expanded form (300 + 50 + 6) and write it directly below 400 + 60 + 7. Point out the importance of lining up the place values vertically.
4. Model how to start with the ones place and work back to the largest place in the problem. Guide students to solve each place value separately, writing the difference to each place out in expanded form (100 + 10 + 1). Then, have students rewrite the difference in standard form. (111)
5. Practice more subtraction without regrouping problems. Have students explain to a partner the steps to subtracting in expanded form.
6. When students are comfortable with this strategy, introduce a problem that requires them to regroup across a place value in expanded form.

 Assess and Extend

Write *78 – 6 =* and *83 – 73 =*. Students should solve the problems and explain which strategy they used to solve each one.

Name _____   Date _____

Subtraction Strategies   ● Comparing Methods

Subtract. Use the number lines for help.

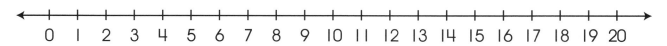

1. 15
     − 8

2. 16
     − 7

3. 18
     − 9

4. 14
     − 9

5. 17
     − 9

6. 17
     − 8

7. 13
     − 6

8. 15
     − 6

9. 16
     − 8

10. 12
      − 7

11. 16
      − 10

12. 14
      − 12

13. 19
      − 11

14. 18
      − 17

15. 20
      − 5

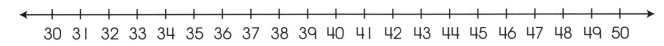

16. 49
      − 19

17. 46
      − 14

18. 38
      − 11

19. 50
      − 12

20. 50
      − 17

21. 39
      − 8

22. 46
      − 13

23. 44
      − 10

24. 50
      − 19

25. 41
      − 11

Subtraction Strategies   ■ Subtraction and the Inverse Operation

Use the inverse operation to write the missing number in each problem.

1. ☐
  − 38
  43

2. ☐
  − 17
  35

3. 460
  − ☐
  281

4. ☐
  − 49
  15

5. 800
  − ☐
  352

6. ☐
  − 24
  49

7. ☐
  − 36
  54

8. ☐
  − 29
  56

9. 856
  − ☐
  569

10. ☐
  − 261
  715

11. ☐
  − 138
  162

12. 600
  − ☐
  459

Name _____   Date _____

Subtraction Strategies ▲ Expanded Form Subtraction

Solve each problem using expanded form. Show your work.

1. 643
    − 412

2. 628
    − 513

3. 667
    − 533

4. 485
    − 252

5. 755
    − 211

6. 851
    − 751

7. 965
    − 222

8. 803
    − 701

Flower Power

Materials: two different colors of crayons or pencils, scrap paper, calculator

To play: Players take turns choosing a subtraction problem. For each problem, the player will solve the problem on scrap paper and tell which strategy he used to find the answer. The other player should use the calculator to check the problem to see if it was solved correctly. For each correct answer, a player should color that petal in his color. The first player to completely color a flower wins.

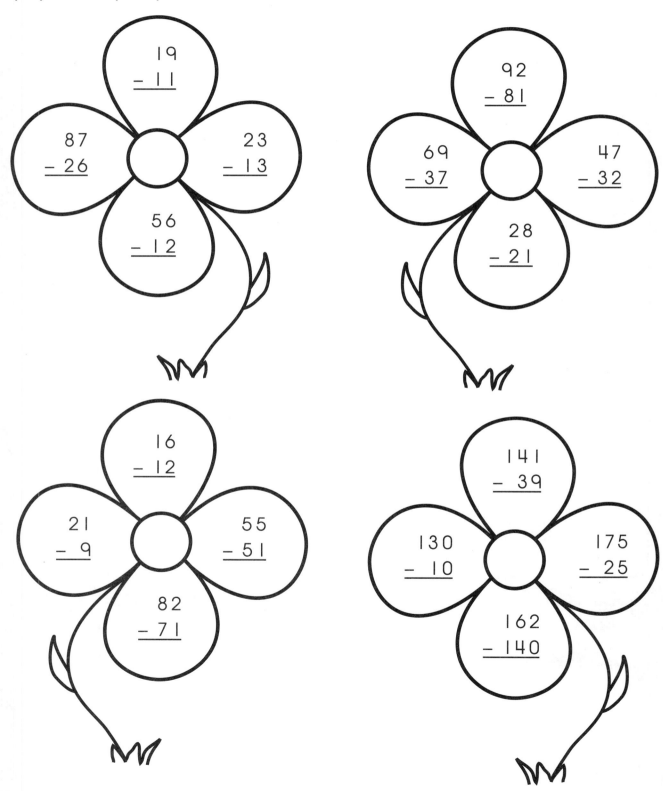

Subtraction with Regrouping

 Essential Question

How is place value used when subtracting with regrouping?

Warm-Up/Review

Write several subtraction problems on the board that do not require regrouping. Have students solve the problems.

 Mini-Lesson

Materials: base ten blocks

1. Write *96 – 18* on the board. Build each number using base ten blocks.

2. Stack the two models and align place values to form a subtraction problem. Remind students to always begin with the ones place and, in subtraction, always subtract from top to bottom in a column.

3. Use ones units to show that you cannot subtract 8 from 6. Use a tens rod from the tens column and model how to exchange it for 10 ones units. Point out that the 9 tens is now 8 tens because you regrouped 1 ten to the ones column. Explain that the value of the number has not changed, and it is now possible to subtract in the ones column.

4. Subtract each column to find the difference. (78)

5. Explain that addition and subtraction are inverse operations—they undo each other. Model how to check your answer by using addition. (78 + 18 = 96)

6. Have students practice building and subtracting numbers with regrouping using base ten blocks.

 Math Talk

When is it necessary to regroup? How do you decide?

Explain how to use base ten blocks to model regrouping.

Is there another way to model regrouping?

 Journal Prompt

Explain why this number sentence is wrong: *34 – 15 = 11*. How do you know it is wrong? Solve the problem correctly.

Materials

base ten blocks

 Workstations

Activity sheets (pages 95–97)
Take Away 15 (page 98)
Flower Power (page 92)

 Guided Math

⬤ **Remediation: Reinforcing the Process**

1. Write *32 – 15*. Incorrectly subtract bottom to top in the ones column and top to bottom in the tens column for a difference of 23. Ask, "How can I check to see if my answer is correct?"

2. Review the use of addition to check subtraction. Write *23 + 15* and find the sum of 38. Point out that 38 and 32 are not the same, so the difference is wrong. Ask students, "Does anyone see what mistake was made?" Explain that 5 ones cannot be taken away from 2 ones without regrouping first, and that you must subtract from top to bottom.

3. Build a base ten model of each number. Ask, "What can I do to make subtracting in the ones column possible?" Remind students that borrowing a rod from the tens place and exchanging it for 10 units does not change the value of the number. Count the total number of base ten blocks after borrowing to verify the number is still 32.

4. Subtract in each column. Practice building and subtracting more numbers using base ten blocks.

5. Have students describe how to solve 41 – 28 using this strategy.

◻ **On Level: Using an Algorithm to Subtract**

1. Provide students with base ten blocks. Write *142 – 114*. Say, "We start the problem with 142 blocks—1 hundred block, 4 tens rods, and 2 ones." Count out the blocks with students.

2. Say, "Then, it says to take away 114. Can you take away 4 from 2?" Model how to regroup 4 tens into 3 tens and 10 ones. After the trade, count all of the blocks, rods, and cubes to show that they still total 142.

3. Demonstrate the process on the equation. "I regrouped one of the tens. That left me with 3 tens." Cross off the 4 and write *3* above it. "I started with 2 ones and now I have 12." Write a *1* beside the 2 in the ones place. Ask, "Can we take away 4 from 12?" Take away 4 ones from 12 and record the difference. Solve the rest of the problem. (28)

4. Have students continue practicing with other equations that require regrouping.

△ **Enrichment: Subtracting Across Zeros**

1. Write *400 – 87* on the board. Draw 4 squares to represent 4 hundreds. Have students copy the problem and picture.

2. Say, "Start with 400. We need to subtract 7 ones and 8 tens. Because we don't have any ones, go to the tens. Are there any tens? Where do we go next? Because there are no tens, regroup one of the hundreds into 10 tens." With students, cross off one of the square blocks and draw 10 lines to represent tens rods. Show on the equation that there are 3 hundreds and 10 tens.

3. Say, "Now, ungroup 1 of the tens into 10 ones." In your drawing, represent the ones units with dots. Show in the problem that there are now 9 tens and 10 ones. Count to confirm that the total is still 400.

4. Have students subtract 8 tens and 7 ones in the model and the algorithm. Write the results of the equation. Read the complete equation.

5. Have students continue practicing with other equations that require multiple regroupings across zeros.

 Assess and Extend

Write *234 – 126 =* and *346 – 229 =* on the board. Have students solve the problems. (108, 117) Then, have students choose one of the problems and explain the steps they took to solve it.

Subtraction with Regrouping   ● Reinforcing the Process

Write the subtraction sentence for each model. Then, find each difference.

1.

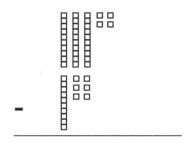

_ _____   _ _____

2.

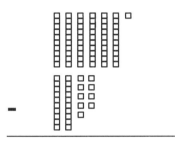

_ _____   _ _____

Subtract. Cross off each answer in the answer bank.

Answer Bank		
14	16	23
27	28	39

3. 35
    − 7
    _____

4. 26
    − 12
    _____

5. 48
    − 21
    _____

6. 57
    − 18
    _____

7. 79
    − 56
    _____

8. 63
    − 47
    _____

Subtraction with Regrouping  Using an Algorithm to Subtract

Subtract. Regroup if necessary.

1.   64
  – 18
	2. 52
	  – 16
		3. 94
		  – 36
			4. 81
			  – 74

5.   70
  – 59
	6. 48
	  – 29
		7. 66
		  – 38
			8. 96
			  – 19

9.   46
  – 27
	10. 84
	  – 36
		11. 80
		  – 64
			12. 78
			  – 9

13.   76
  – 29
	14. 44
	  – 18
		15. 56
		  – 37
			16. 54
			  – 46

17.   62
  – 57
	18. 49
	  – 22
		19. 88
		  – 59
			20. 98
			  – 17

Subtraction with Regrouping ▲ Subtracting Across Zeros

Subtract. Use a drawing to show your work.

1. $\begin{array}{r} 30 \\ -\ 18 \\ \hline \end{array}$	**2.** $\begin{array}{r} 90 \\ -\ 22 \\ \hline \end{array}$
3. $\begin{array}{r} 40 \\ -\ 11 \\ \hline \end{array}$	**4.** $\begin{array}{r} 80 \\ -\ 35 \\ \hline \end{array}$
5. $\begin{array}{r} 70 \\ -\ 46 \\ \hline \end{array}$	**6.** $\begin{array}{r} 400 \\ -\ 23 \\ \hline \end{array}$
7. $\begin{array}{r} 500 \\ -\ 124 \\ \hline \end{array}$	**8.** $\begin{array}{r} 900 \\ -\ 368 \\ \hline \end{array}$

Take Away 15

Materials: I die, scrap paper, two colors of counters, calculator

To play: Players take turns. Place the counters on START. Roll the die and move that many spaces. Subtract 15 from the number landed on. Use scrap paper if needed to solve. Partners should use the calculator to check each other's answers. If the answer is not correct, the player loses a turn. The first player to reach FINISH wins the game.

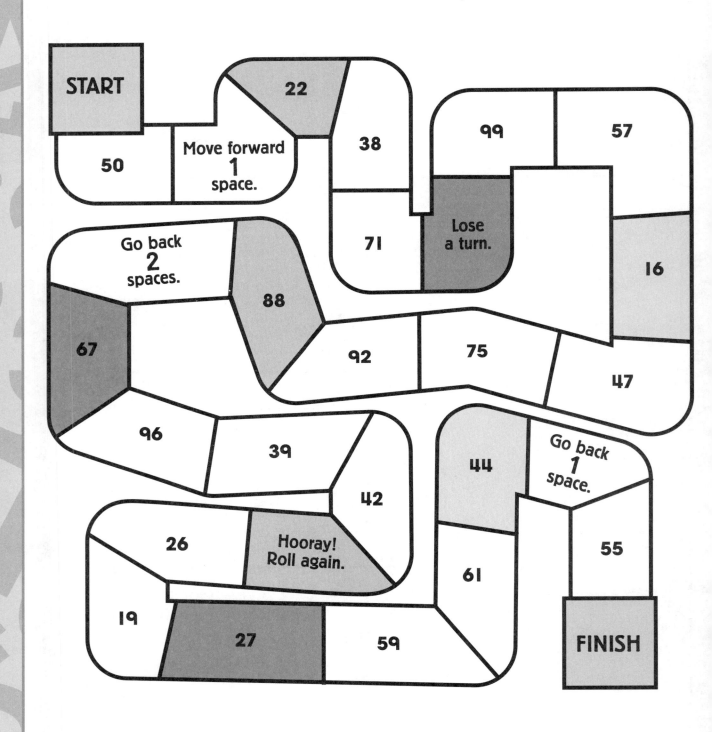

Mental Math (10 and 100)

Essential Question

How can mental math help with addition and subtraction?

Warm-Up/Review

Give each student a hundred chart. Say a number, such as 67, and challenge students to use the chart to find 10 more or 10 less. Repeat several times with different numbers. As a class, discuss what strategies students used to quickly find 10 more or 10 less.

Mini-Lesson

Materials: two sheets of blank paper, hundred chart

1. Write *76 + 10* on the board vertically. Cover both numbers in the tens column with a sheet of paper. Ask, "How much is 6 + 0?" Write the answer.

2. Move the paper to the ones column, covering both numbers. Say, "How much is 7 + 1?" Complete the problem.

3. Repeat with several more problems, both with addition and subtraction. (In subtraction, discuss how the number in the tens place counts 1 down.) Ask, "What pattern can you see between the addend and the sum?" (The number in the tens place counts up 1, the number in the ones place stays the same.) Model the movement on a hundred chart to show how the number is directly above or below the number in the tens place.

4. Repeat steps 1 through 3 with a 3-digit addend plus 100.

5. Explain how the number in the hundreds place counts up 1 and the numbers in the tens and ones places stay the same. Repeat with several more problems, with both addition and subtraction. (In subtraction, discuss how the number in the hundreds place counts 1 down.)

6. Discuss how students should mentally visualize this process when thinking about adding or subtracting 10 or 100 to a number.

Math Talk

When you add/subtract 10 to/from a 2-digit number, what happens to the number in the tens place? Why?

When you add/subtract 100 to/from a 3-digit number, what happens to the number in the hundreds place? Why?

Why is it important to know how to use mental math?

Journal Prompt

Describe some instances where you have used mental math or would need to know mental math.

Materials

base ten blocks
hundred chart
blank number lines with 10 tick marks

 Workstations

Activity sheets (pages 101–103)
Numbers Back and Forth
(page 104)

 Guided Math

⬤ **Remediation: Modeling Addition and Subtraction**

1. Distribute base ten blocks to students. Write *36 + 10* and *36 – 10*.
2. Have students show 36 with their blocks. Say, "Add a ten. Now, how many do you have?" Then, have students show 36 again. Say, "Now take away a ten. Now, how many do you have?"
3. Have students show 36 again. Say, "Now we will add a hundred to some numbers. Add a hundred to your blocks. Now, how many do you have?" (136) Write the number sentence *100 + 36 = 136* and explain how it relates to what students just did.
4. Write *125 + 100 = ?*. Have students show 125 with base ten blocks. Ask, "What are you adding to 125? How would we show that? What is the sum of 125 and 100?" Repeat the activity and subtract 100 from 125.
5. Have students discuss what happens in the tens and hundreds places when adding and subtracting 10 or 100.

◻ **On Level: Visualizing with Patterns**

1. Draw a number line marked from 78 to 978 in increments of 100. Draw curved lines connecting each number on the number line and write *+100* above each curve. Have students count aloud as you draw and mark each curve.
2. Draw a number line marked from 43 to 943 in increments of 100. Start at the right end of the number line. Draw curved lines above the numbers as before and mark *–100* as you count back.
3. Practice adding and subtracting more tens and hundreds on the number line. Discuss how adding and subtracting 10 and 100 on a number line relates to skip counting.
4. Distribute blank number lines with 10 tick marks. Have students mark a pattern of +100 or –100 on their number lines with various numbers, leaving some of the numbers blank. Have students exchange number lines with a partner and fill in the blank spaces. Students should return the number lines and check to see if they are correct.
5. Have students practice writing number sentences (100 + ___ = ___) using their number lines.

△ **Enrichment: Real-World Mental Math**

1. Pose the following problem: *If I have 396 trading cards and my friend gives me 10 more, how many trading cards will I have?*
2. Discuss and share possible strategies for mentally solving the problem. Say, "We still have to focus on the tens place. If you have 9 tens and then one more ten, you now have 10 tens. Ten 10s is the same as 100 so you must add the 100 to the 300, leaving you with 4 hundreds, 0 tens, and 6 ones." (406)
3. Pose another problem: *My family is going to the amusement park next week. The total price of the tickets for 5 family members is $500. Now, my uncle would also like to come with us. Our budget is $600. Will we have enough money?*
4. Discuss and share possible answers to the word problem. Then, model the steps to mentally solve the problem.
5. Have students write a realistic word problem involving adding or subtracting 100 and exchange with a partner to solve. Encourage students to use mental math to solve the word problems.

 Assess and Extend

Write *278 – 100 =* and *566 + 100 =* on the board. Have students use mental math to solve the problems. Then, have students choose one of the problems and explain the steps they took to solve it.

Mental Math (10 and 100)   ● Modeling Addition and Subtraction

Use base ten blocks to help you solve each problem. The first one has been done for you.

1. 51 – 10 = __41__ 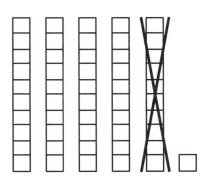	**2.** 133 + 10 = _____
3. 120 + 100 = _____	**4.** 387 – 10 = _____
5. 432 + 100 = _____	**6.** 299 – 100 = _____

Mental Math (10 and 100)

Look at each number in the middle column. Write the number that is 100 less and the number that is 100 more.

100 Less	100 More		100 Less	100 More
1. _____ 206 _____			2. _____ 765 _____	
3. _____ 413 _____			4. _____ 888 _____	
5. _____ 307 _____			6. _____ 844 _____	
7. _____ 130 _____			8. _____ 371 _____	
9. _____ 662 _____			10. _____ 222 _____	
11. _____ 440 _____			12. _____ 628 _____	
13. _____ 330 _____			14. _____ 264 _____	
15. _____ 290 _____			16. _____ 549 _____	
17. _____ 631 _____			18. _____ 870 _____	
19. _____ 808 _____			20. _____ 900 _____	

Mental Math (10 and 100)   ▲ Real-World Mental Math

Use mental math to solve each problem.

1. Peter read 100 pages on Saturday. He read 56 pages on Sunday. How many more pages did Peter read all weekend?

_____ pages

2. Carlos counted 200 books in his classroom. Troy counted 88 books. How many books did they count in all?

_____ books

3. Jasmine read for 63 minutes in the morning. After lunch, she read for 100 minutes. Before she went to bed, she read for 10 minutes. How many minutes did Jasmine read altogether?

_____ minutes

4. Megan bought a book with 315 pages. She has read 215 pages. How many pages does she have left?

_____ pages

5. Mark counted 397 words in his book. Andy counted 197 words in his book. How many more words are in Mark's book?

_____ words

6. Grant has read 200 books from the library. Jason has read 125 books. How many books have they read in all?

_____ books

Numbers Back and Forth

Materials: two colors of counters, sharpened pencil, paper clip, laminated hundred and thousand charts

To play: Each player places a counter on the chart on the top-left square of the chart they are using (hundred or thousand). Players take turns using the sharpened pencil and paper clip to spin the spinner. Players move their counters according to the number they spin. If a player cannot add or subtract a number, she loses a turn. The winner is the first person to move her counter to 100 (or 1,000) or to the greatest number when time runs out.

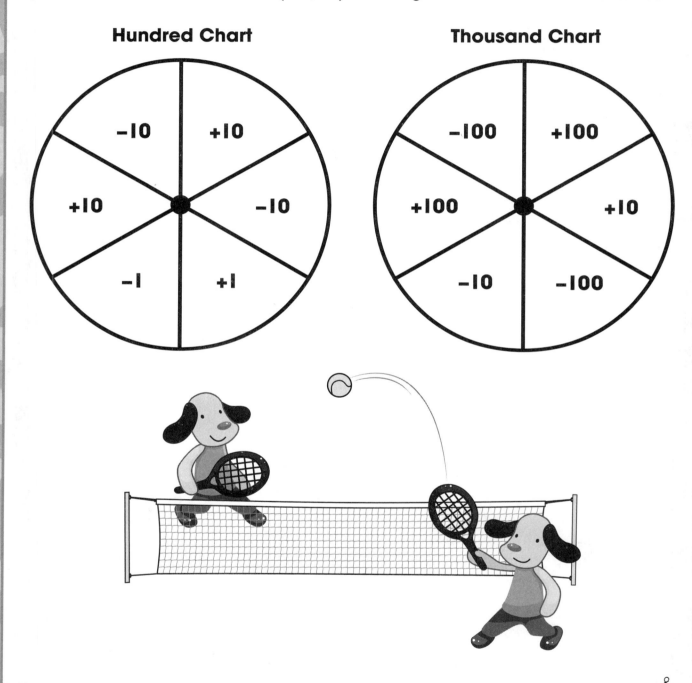

Hundred Chart

Thousand Chart

To prep: Copy on card stock and laminate for durability. Print or copy large hundred and thousand charts on cardstock and laminate for durability. Place the charts in the center with the directions and spinners. Cut off these directions before copying.

Comparing Units of Measurement

 Essential Question

How does using a different unit change a measurement?

 Warm-Up/Review

Display a yardstick, a meterstick, a ruler, and a tape measure. Ask students to tell you what they notice about each measurement tool. (One answer may be that they all have numbers on them.)

 Mini-Lesson

Materials: objects of various sizes (see below), measurement tools from Warm-Up/Review activity

1. Display different objects at the front of the class. Show tall, short, heavy, and light objects.

2. Ask students to describe the objects in terms of their size and compare them to each other. Write the statements on the board.

3. Ask, "How can we describe the sizes of the objects in a more specific way?" Have students brainstorm standard measurements (inch, centimeter, feet, meters, etc.) and record a list on the board.

4. Challenge students to match their general descriptions of the objects with the appropriate standard measurement units that could be used to describe the objects instead. For example, *the door is tall so it could be measured in units of feet or meters.*

5. Ask, "Would we use meters to measure a paper clip? Would we use inches to measure the door? Would we use centimeters to measure a car?" Have students discuss their answers with a partner.

 Math Talk

Why is it important to know which kind of measurement tool to use when measuring an object?
How do you know which tool to use?
Could you use a different unit? Which one? Why?

 Journal Prompt

Compare a yardstick with a tape measure. What is the same about them? What is different about them?

Materials

measurement tools (yardsticks, metersticks, inch and centimeter rulers, tape measures)
tool and unit index cards (see below)
masking tape

 Workstations

Activity sheets (pages 107–109)
Roll and Cover Three-in-a-Row (page 110)

 Guided Math

⚪ **Remediation: Measurement Tools**

1. Provide a variety of measurement tools, such as yardsticks, metersticks, rulers, and tape measures, for students to examine. Discuss the purpose of each tool and its units.
2. Make several sets of matching index cards printed with names of measurement tools and units of measure. For example, a *ruler* card and a *centimeters* card or a *tape measure* card and an *inches* card. (There should be one match for each tool.)
3. Allow students to play a matching memory game with the cards.
4. Ask students to discuss the prompt, "Why are there different tools for different units of measurement?"

⬜ **On Level: Comparing Measurements**

1. Explain to students that some units of measurement are best for measuring large things and some are best for measuring small things.
2. Make sets of unit cards by writing units of measurement on index cards. Include both customary unit cards (*inches* and *feet*) and metric unit cards (*centimeters* and *meters*).
3. Divide a table in half with masking tape and label the halves *large* and *small*. Have students place each unit card under the correct heading.
4. Have students order each set (standard and metric) from the smallest to the largest unit. Ask, "Which metric unit would you use to measure the height of a tree? (meter) Which measurement makes more sense for the length of a room: 15 inches or 15 feet?" (15 feet)
5. Ask students to discuss the prompt, "Why do we need different units of measurement?"

🔺 **Enrichment: Estimating Measurements**

1. Give each student an inch ruler. Have them find a parts of their hands that are about 1 inch long (width of a thumb or length of a section of finger) and a parts of their arms that are about 1 foot long (length of a forearm with or without hand).
2. Explain that it can be useful when you do not have a ruler handy to have a reference for estimating lengths. You may also wish to have students choose a referent for centimeters, such as the width of their pinky finger.
3. Provide students with several classroom objects to measure using their estimation referents.
4. Ask, "About how long is my desk? Which object is about 8 feet long?" After students have made their estimates, help them check their measurements using standard measurement tools.
5. Ask students to discuss the prompt, "When might you need to estimate measurements?"

 Assess and Extend

Post several pictures of objects, such as a car, a dress, a door, a rug, etc., on the board. Number the objects. Then, have students tell which measurement tool would be best to measure the length of each object.

Comparing Units of Measurement 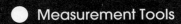 ● Measurement Tools

Circle the best tool for measuring each object.

1.

ruler   tape measure

2.

ruler   tape measure

3.

ruler   tape measure

4.

tape measure   meterstick

5.

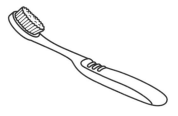

yardstick   ruler

6.

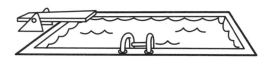

ruler   meterstick

7.

yardstick   ruler

8.

meterstick   ruler

Comparing Units of Measurement

Circle the smaller measurement.

1. 3 centimeters   or   3 inches

2. 6 yards   or   6 feet

3. 20 feet   or   20 inches

4. 1 meter   or   1 yard

Circle the best measurement for each object.

5.   5 feet   5 inches

6.   10 feet   10 inches

7.   7 meters   7 centimeters

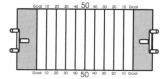

8.   100 yards   100 feet

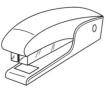

9.   6 inches   6 centimeters

10.   15 feet   15 meters

Comparing Units of Measurement   ▲ Estimating Measurements

Read each problem. Answer the question.

1. Macy's mother was painting a wall in her bedroom. She asked Macy and her brother to bring her one of the ladders from the garage. There was a 5-foot ladder and a 14-foot ladder. Which ladder should they bring her? Why?

_____

_____

_____

2. Ben got a yardstick to measure his pencil. Is this a good choice? Why or why not?

_____

_____

_____

3. Tasha wanted to measure her jump rope. Which tool would be the best for measuring it, a tape measure or a ruler? Why?

_____

_____

_____

4. Tarik wanted to measure his sleeping bag. His friend says he can measure it with a meterstick or a yardstick. Is he right? Why or why not?

_____

_____

_____

Roll and Cover Three-in-a-Row

Materials: 1 die, two colors of counters

To play: Players take turns. Player 1 rolls the die, and uses the key at the top of the page to find his unit. Then, he should find an item on the playing board that can be measured with that unit of measurement. (Some items can be measured with more than one unit.) The player should cover the item with a counter. The first player to have three pictures covered in a row on their board (horizontally, diagonally, or vertically) wins the round.

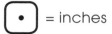

- = inches
- = feet
- = FREE
- = meters
- = centimeters
- = yards

Player 1
Round 1

Player 2
Round 1

Round 2

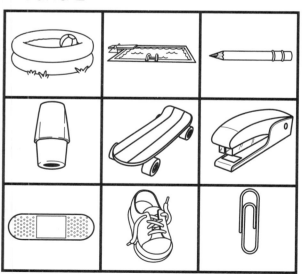

Round 2

- ✂

To prep: Copy on card stock and laminate for durability. Cut off these directions before copying.

Measuring Length

 Essential Question

How do we measure an object?

Warm-Up/Review

Have students measure the widths of their desks by lining paper clips end to end across the top. Students should count the paper clips to get a final measurement. Then, have students repeat the activity again using markers lined up end to end. Discuss why the final measurement was different.

 Mini-Lesson

Materials: inch and centimeter rulers, yardstick, tape measure

1. Distribute rulers to students. Examine an inch ruler together. Then, display the yardstick and tape measure. Point out the inch marks on all of the measurement tools. Explain that rulers are made with the exact same measurements so that comparisons are consistent. If using the length of a human foot to measure, for example, lengths would vary and depend on the size of the foot. Compare your shoe to a student's and point out the difference. If desired, use both shoes to measure the same distance. Because measurement units are standard, comparisons are more accurate.

2. Point out how the inch marks are exactly spaced and the unit marks between the numbers show parts of an inch. Compare this with the centimeter ruler. Explain that some countries use the customary system (inches), while other countries use the metric system (centimeters).

3. Model how to measure an object. Line up the first line (0) on the ruler with the end of an object. Always start with the number 0, not the number 1, like when counting on a number line.

4. Have students practice measuring objects in the classroom with both the inch and centimeter rulers.

 Math Talk

Why is it important to be accurate in measuring?

What may happen if you use the wrong label to describe your measurement?

How many inches long is this object? Will there be more or less centimeters? How do you know?

 Journal Prompt

Find an object in the room. List the steps you would take to measure it. Include the unit of measurement and the measurement tool you would use.

Materials

centimeter and inch rulers
chart paper

 Workstations

Activity sheets (pages 113–115)
Measuring Ups and Downs
    (page 116)
Roll and Cover Three-in-a-Row
    (page 110)

 Guided Math

◯ **Remediation: Reinforcing Technique**

1. Review the difference between the customary and metric systems of measurement.

2. Look at the unit marks on a ruler. Point out that the inch marks are spaced exactly the same distance apart. Compare the customary and metric system rulers. Ask, "How many units does a customary ruler show? (12 in.) How many units does a metric ruler show?" (About 30 cm)

3. Model how to line up the first line on the inch ruler with the end of a classroom object. Remind students to always start with 0. Say, "Think of rulers like a number line. Just like with a number line, you begin counting with 0, not 1." Lay the ruler on a flat surface with the object and find its measurement. Model rounding to the nearest whole inch.

4. Follow the same steps to measure objects in centimeters to the nearest whole centimeter. Allow students to practice measuring other objects. Emphasize the ease and accuracy in comparison with using nonstandard units.

▢ **On Level: Practicing Measuring**

1. Compare a customary and metric ruler. Ask, "How many inches are on a customary ruler? How many centimeters are on a metric ruler? Are the centimeter units larger or smaller than the inch units? About how many centimeters are in one inch?"

2. Model how to measure a classroom object, like a pencil, in inches. Remind students how to line up a ruler. Explain that if a measurement is rounded to the nearest whole or another increment, they should say the object is "about" that many units.

3. Introduce the measurement abbreviations for inches (in.) and centimeters (cm). Ask, "Does it make a difference if I forget to write the unit label after the measurement? How does the label affect the measurement?"

4. Draw a straight line on chart paper. Ask volunteers to measure the length with both rulers. Encourage students to explain their thought processes, describe their measurements, and compare the units.

△ **Enrichment: Practical Measuring**

1. Compare a customary and metric ruler. Ask, "How many inches are on a customary ruler? How many centimeters are on a metric ruler? Are the centimeter units larger or smaller than the inch units? About how many centimeters are in one inch?"

2. Draw lines of various lengths, including those that are not whole-unit lengths and those that are longer than 12 inches. Invite volunteers to measure the lengths with both rulers. Challenge students to deal with in-between measurements and lengths greater than 12 inches. Ask, "Should I round up or down? Can I use a half-inch? How can I use the same ruler to measure a line that is longer than the ruler?"

3. Model how to draw a line of a given length (5 cm). Label the line with the correct unit.

4. Let students practice drawing lines of differing lengths. Direct students to switch their lines with partners to measure and label the lines.

 Assess and Extend

Assign several classroom objects, such as crayons, paper clips, books, etc., for students to measure with a ruler, in both centimeters and inches. Have them record their measurements. Check the measurements for accuracy.

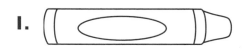 **Measuring Length**   Reinforcing Technique

Measure each object to the nearest whole unit. Write the length in inches and centimeters.

1. 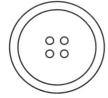 _____ in.

   _____ cm

2.   _____ in.

   _____ cm

3. 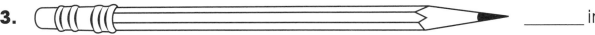 _____ in.

   _____ cm

4. 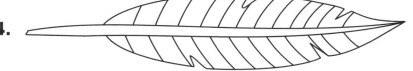 _____ in.

   _____ cm

5.  _____ in.

   _____ cm

6.  _____ in.

   _____ cm

7. 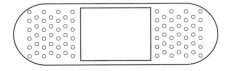 _____ in.

   _____ cm

8.  _____ in.

   _____ cm

Measuring Length ☐ Practicing Measuring

Circle the more reasonable length for each object. Measure each object to the nearest inch or centimeter.

1.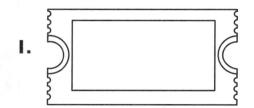

2 inches or 2 centimeters?

Actual: _____

2.

4 inches or 4 centimeters?

Actual: _____

3.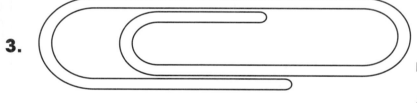

4 inches or 4 centimeters?

Actual: _____

4.

3 inches or 3 centimeters?

Actual: _____

5.

2 inches or 2 centimeters?

Actual: _____

6.

3 inches or 3 centimeters?

Actual: _____

Measuring Length ▲ Practical Measuring

Draw a line to match the given measurement. Then, answer the questions.

1. 4 in.

2. 8 cm

3. 2 in.

4. 3 in.

5. 5 cm

6. 4 cm

7. $5\frac{1}{2}$ in.

8. 6 cm

9. How many times would you have to move your ruler to measure an object that was 30 inches long?

_____

_____

10. How many times would you have to move your ruler to measure an object that was 30 centimeters long?

_____

_____

Measuring Ups and Downs

Materials: I die, two colors of counters, inch and centimeter ruler, objects pictured below

To play: Place the counters on the Start space. Players take turns. Roll the die and move that number of spaces. Measure the real object to the nearest unit given. Players should check each other's measurements for accuracy. If a player lands on a ladder, he should move his counter up the ladder. The object does not have to be measured to stay on the space. If a player lands on a slide, he moves his counter down the slide and loses his turn. Continue until one player reaches the Finish space.

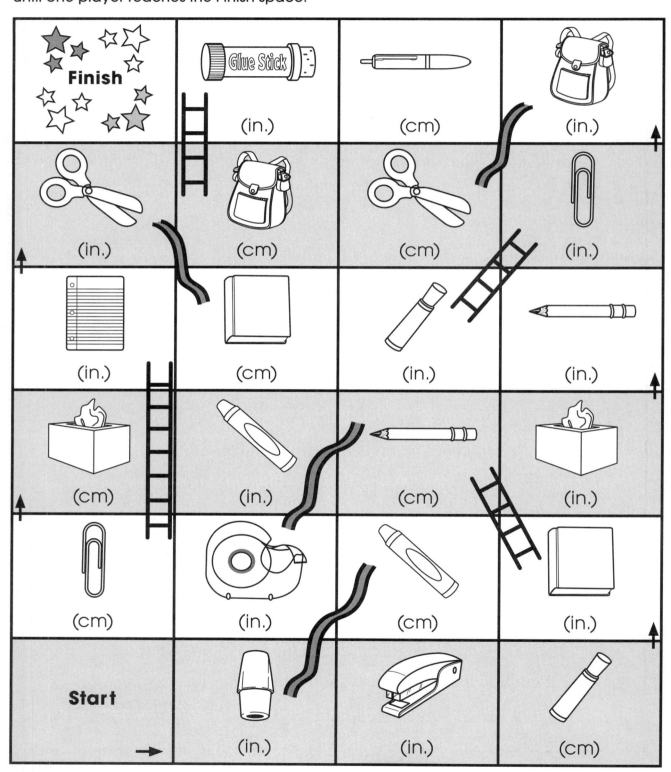

Estimating Length

? Essential Question

How can estimating length help solve real-world problems?

◐ Warm-Up/Review

Review the terms *length*, *inches*, *centimeters*, *feet*, *yards*, and *meters*. Then, have students measure objects in the classroom with different units of measurement.

★ Mini-Lesson

Materials: index cards preprogrammed with various length estimates

1. Define the term *estimate*. Say, "When we use estimation in measuring length, we are using previous knowledge to figure out what the length of something might be. It is not just a guess."

2. Have each student look at the board. Have them think about estimating the length of the board. Ask, "Do we really have to measure it, or can we think of a length that would come close? Would knowing the correct unit help us to estimate the length? Would we want to use a standard or nonstandard measurement unit? Why?" Emphasize that measuring something in centimeters would be very different than measuring something in feet or meters.

3. For each pair of students, distribute an index card that is preprogrammed with an estimate, such as *around 16 centimeters long*, *about 4 feet tall*, or *almost 6 inches long*. Have students read their estimates and then write the name of an object in the classroom that would best fit the estimate. Review the estimates as a class. Then, allow students to measure their objects and write the actual measurements.

4. Have students exchange index cards and repeat the activity. Students should choose and measure a different object in the classroom.

💬 Math Talk

How is estimating different than finding an exact measurement?
When might you need to use estimation when measuring length?
Explain estimating to a friend.

✎ Journal Prompt

Jack said his teacher is about 15 feet tall. Anna said that was wrong and that their teacher is about 6 feet tall. Which estimate is more reasonable? Explain how you know.

Materials

book
rulers
various objects to measure

 Workstations

Activity sheets (pages 119–121)
Estimation Station (page 122)
Measuring Ups and Downs
(page 116)

 Guided Math

◯ **Remediation: Hands-On Estimation**

1. Display a book. Say, "Do you think I should use centimeters or meters to measure this book? (centimeters) Is there another unit of measure that we could use? (inches) Why would I not use feet or meters to measure this book?" (Students should recognize that meters or feet are too large to measure the book, and that a smaller unit is needed.)

2. Hold up the book. Have students estimate how many centimeters tall the book is from top to bottom. As a group, review the answers and discuss any misconceptions. Repeat the activity and have students estimate using inches.

3. Have a volunteer measure the book's height in both centimeters and inches. Review and discuss students' answers to check for understanding.

4. Have students choose a book, estimate the length, and then record the actual measurement. Repeat with other items around the classroom.

◻ **On Level: Estimates and Measures**

1. Have students choose 10 items in the classroom to measure. Students should choose at least two objects to represent each unit of measure (inches, feet, centimeters, yards, and meters).

2. Have students estimate the lengths of the objects they have chosen and record the estimates. Ask, "Does your estimate seem reasonable? Why or why not?"

3. Have students measure each object and record the measurement to the nearest whole number. Ask, "How did you decide what tool to use?"

4. Discuss the estimates and the actual measurements of the students' objects, making sure the unit of measurement is labeled beside each actual measurement.

△ **Enrichment: Visualizing Estimation**

1. Give a ruler to each student and have them lay them flat. Ask, "Can you close your eyes and visualize an inch?" Have students show a space between their thumb and forefinger to demonstrate what they estimate to be the size of an inch. Say, "Now, without changing the distance between your fingers, measure the space between your fingers with the ruler and see if you estimated an inch correctly." Repeat the activity with visualizing the space between two hands to demonstrate a foot.

2. Have students look at the length of the classroom. Say, "I would estimate the length of the classroom to be 20 feet long. Do you think that is a reasonable estimate?" Encourage students to use their visualization of a ruler as a measurement of one foot. Discuss the answers. Measure the length of the classroom to confirm the estimate. Then, ask, "What do you think the length of the room is in meters? In yards?" Discuss students' answers and measure in both units to confirm the estimations.

3. Give students several objects around the room to estimate the length of in inches, centimeters, feet, yards, and meters. Then, have them measure the objects and compare the estimated lengths with the actual lengths. Have students calculate the difference.

 Assess and Extend

Assign various objects to students to estimate length and then measure in inches, centimeters, feet, meters, and yards.

▦ Estimating Length   ● Hands-On Estimation

Estimate the length of each line. Record your estimate. Measure the line in inches or centimeters. Record the actual length.

1. ──────

    I think the line is _____ **inches** long.   Actual: _____ in.

2. ─────

    I think the line is _____ **centimeters** long.   Actual: _____ cm

3. ──────────────────────────

    I think the line is _____ **inches** long.   Actual: _____ in.

4. ──────────

    I think the line is _____ **centimeters** long.   Actual: _____ cm

5. ────────────────────────────

    I think the line is _____ **inches** long.   Actual: _____ in.

6. ─────────────────

    I think the line is _____ **inches** long.   Actual: _____ in.

7. ───────────

    I think the line is _____ **centimeters** long.   Actual: _____ cm

8. ───────────────

    I think the line is _____ **centimeters** long.   Actual: _____ cm

Estimating Length

Estimates and Measures

Estimate the length of each line in inches or centimeters. Measure the lines. Record the actual measurement. Write each length.

	Estimate	**Actual**

1. _____

_____ in.   _____ in.

2. _____

_____ cm   _____ cm

3. _____

_____ in.   _____ in.

4. _____

_____ cm   _____ cm

5. _____

_____ cm   _____ cm

6. _____

_____ in.   _____ in.

7. _____

_____ cm   _____ cm

Draw a line to match the given measurement.

8. 6 inches

9. 17 centimeters

10. 8 inches

Estimating Length   ▲ Visualizing Estimation

Estimate the length of each line in inches or centimeters. Measure the lines. Record the actual measurement. Write each length.

I. Look at each line from the spider to the web. How far is each distance?

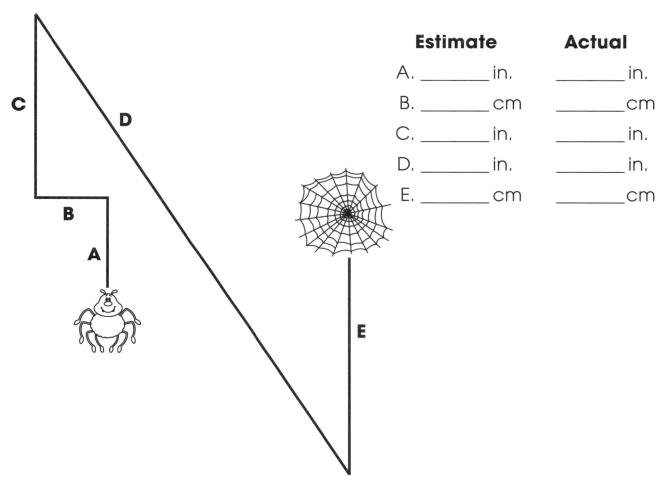

	Estimate	**Actual**
A.	_____ in.	_____ in.
B.	_____ cm	_____ cm
C.	_____ in.	_____ in.
D.	_____ in.	_____ in.
E.	_____ cm	_____ cm

Draw a line to match the given measurement.

2. 14 centimeters

3. 8 centimeters

4. 7 inches

5. 2 inches

Estimation Station

Materials: inch and centimeter rulers, objects pictured below

To play: Look at each real-life object. Each player estimates the length of it and records their estimate. Then, measure the object and record the actual measurement. Color the box of the player that got the closest. The player with the most colored boxes wins.

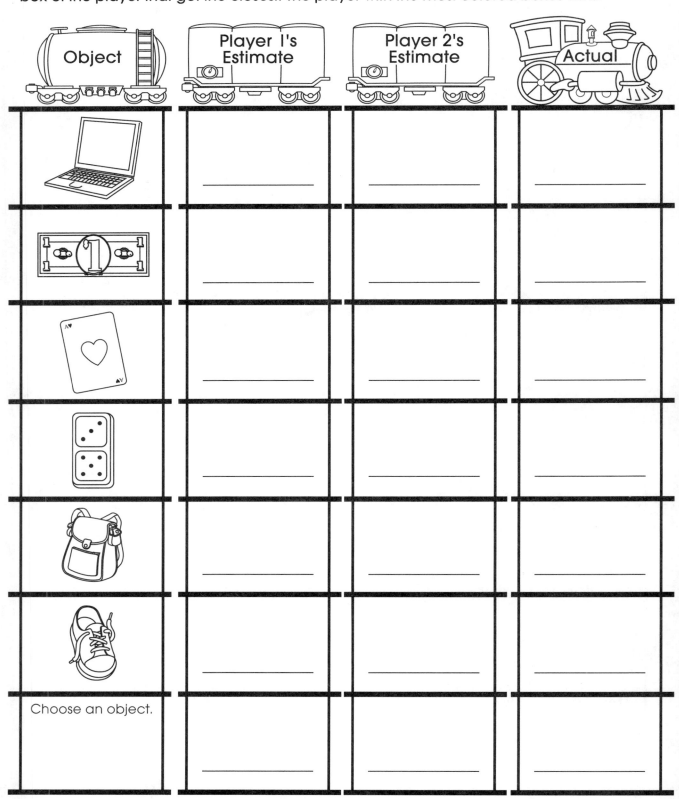

Object	Player 1's Estimate	Player 2's Estimate	Actual
Choose an object.			

Measurement Word Problems

 Essential Question

How can measurement problems be solved using addition and subtraction?

 Warm-Up/Review

Display a ruler. Ask, "How is a ruler like a number line?" Explain that they both show numbers in order and that the numbers are equally spaced. Display a number line and review using it to add and subtract.

 Mini-Lesson

Materials: copies of a word problem (see below), laminated number lines, dry-erase markers

1. Read the following problem: *Jamie wants to put a candy ribbon along the outside of her rectangular cake. The candy ribbon is 36 inches long. Her cake is 7 inches long and 5 inches wide. Does she have enough candy ribbon?* Provide a copy to each student.

2. Remind students of the process of solving a word problem. Say, "What is the problem asking you to find? What information do you have? Can you use a drawing or a number line to help you?"

3. Have students draw a rectangle with sides labeled *5 inches*, *7 inches*, *5 inches*, and *7 inches*. Model how to add the four sides together. (5 + 7 + 5 + 7 = 24 inches).

4. Ask, "Does Jamie have enough candy ribbon? How much does she have left over?" Draw a straight arrow (or bar) to the number 24 on the top of a number line to demonstrate how to show 24 inches. Then, draw another arrow (or bar) to model 36 inches. Ask students what they notice about the two arrows. Have students count back from 36 to 24 to discover that Jamie has 12 inches of candy ribbon left over.

5. Present another measurement word problem such as: *Shane has 26 meters of rope. He used 14 meters of the rope to tie his boat up. How many meters of rope does Shane still have?* (12 meters) Have students work in pairs to solve the problem. Students should discuss different strategies they could use to solve the problem.

 Math Talk

What are you solving for? How do you know?
Why did you choose to do that first?
Could you solve this another way? How?

 Journal Prompt

Why is it important to know the correct measurements of objects when you are building something?

Materials

copies of word problems (see below)
sentence strips
highlighters

 Workstations

Activity sheets (pages 125–127)
Silly Stories (page 128)
Estimation Station (page 122)

 Guided Math

○ **Remediation: Strategies to Solve Length Problems**

1. Display the following problem: *Ms. Wallace decorated her room with 12 meters of ribbon on Monday. On Tuesday, she decorated with 6 more meters of ribbon than she used on Monday. How many meters of ribbon did Ms. Wallace use to decorate in all this week?*

2. Draw a bar on the board labeled *M* for Monday and write *12 m* inside the bar. Say, "When did Ms. Wallace decorate again? Did she use less or more ribbon than Monday?" Draw a longer bar under the first one and label it *T* for Tuesday. Draw a question mark inside the bar. Ask, "Do we know how much more she used on Tuesday? We know that she used 6 meters more than Monday, so we can add 12 m + 6 m to equal 18 m." Replace the question mark with *18 m*.

3. Ask, "Can we find the total amount of ribbon that Ms. Wallace used now?" Have students discuss their strategies.

4. Write the number sentence *18 + 12 = 30*. Say, "Ms. Wallace used 30 meters of ribbon in all."

5. Ask students what other strategies could be used to solve this problem. Then, model how to use a number line to solve the problem.

☐ **On Level: Modeling Perimeter Word Problems**

1. Read the following word problem: *Mr. Chang has a garden that is 2 feet by 3 feet. He wants to put a wooden fence around the outside of the garden to keep out the rabbits. How many feet of fencing will he need?* Give each student a copy of the problem.

2. Use sentence strips cut into 2 feet and 3 feet sections to make a large rectangle on the floor. Label the top and bottom sections *2 feet*. Label the left and right side pieces *3 feet*. Ask, "How would you figure out the distance around this garden?" Have students share their ideas.

3. Have a volunteer start at one corner and walk around each side of the rectangle while the group counts out loud to help her keep track of how many feet she has traveled.

4. Discuss how to find distance around an object by adding all of the sides. Model this by placing the sentence strips end to end. Add the lengths of each side. (3 feet + 2 feet + 3 feet + 2 feet = 10 feet). Write the addition sentence on the board. Ask students to solve the word problem.

△ **Enrichment: Writing and Solving Measurement Word Problems**

1. Write *30 inches – ? inches = 3 inches* on the board.

2. Ask students to imagine a word problem to describe the equation. Discuss how the word problem must make sense with the units. Provide a copy of the following to students: *A beetle is climbing a fence post. It is 3 inches from the top. If the fence post is 30 inches tall, how far has the beetle climbed so far?* Have students use their word problem strategies, including highlighting key words, to solve the problem. (27 inches)

3. Have students write their own word problems for the same equation. Share and discuss students' word problems. Have students identify the clues in each problem that would help them solve the problem.

4. Continue writing word problems for additional equations, including those for multi-step problems.

 Assess and Extend

Have students solve the following problem: *Ava was making a bracelet out of beads. The first time she measured the bracelet, it was 3 inches long. She added 2 more inches of beads. Then, an inch of beads fell off of the string. Finally, she added 3 more inches of beads. How long is Ava's bracelet?*

Name _____   Date _____

Solve each word problem using the number line.

1. Kelly had 17 feet of ribbon. She gave Chris 6 feet. How much ribbon does she have left? _____ feet

2. Paul had 18 meters of fishing line. Then, 9 meters broke off. How many meters are left? _____ meters

3. Dante has 8 yards of kite string. He needs 12 more yards. How many yards does he need altogether? _____ yards

4. Before Mateo sharpened his pencil, it was 16 centimeters long. After he sharpened it, it was 13 centimeters long. How many centimeters longer was the pencil before he sharpened it?

_____ centimeters

5. Ms. Sanchez bought a garden hose that was 10 feet long. She has a garden hose that is 8 feet long. When she puts them together, what will the new length of the garden hose be? _____ feet

Measurement Word Problems

Draw a number line to solve each problem.

1. Cole had 27 feet of wire. He gave Dante 8 feet. How much wire does Cole have left?

0 1 2 3 4 5 6 7 8 9 10 11 12 13 14 15 16 17 18 19 20 21 22 23 24 25 26 27 28 29 30

_____ feet

2. Emily had 41 yards of string to fly a kite. The string broke and Emily had only 20 yards of string left. How many yards of string broke?

_____ yards

3. Lily has a 14-centimeter piece of trim to put on a dress. She needs 14 more centimeters of trim to finish the dress. How many inches does she need altogether?

_____ centimeters

4. Jorge wants to plant sunflowers around the outside of his garden. His garden is 4 feet by 4 feet. How many total feet of sunflowers will Jorge plant in his garden?

_____ feet

5. Olivia walked 27 meters on Saturday. Mason walked 18 more meters than Olivia on Sunday. How many meters did Mason walk on Sunday?

_____ meters

🟫 Measurement Word Problems ▲ Writing and Solving Measurement Word Problems

Solve each word problem. Show your work with number lines, number sentences, pictures, or words.

1. Amy had a haircut. The stylist cut off 5 inches. Now, her hair is 12 inches long. How long was Amy's hair before the haircut?

2. Pedro bought a new 25-meter hose. It is 10 meters longer than his old hose. How many feet long was Pedro's old hose?

3. Ingrid needs 42 yards of yarn to make a scarf. She has already used 33 yards. How many more yards does Ingrid need to finish her scarf?

Write a measurement word problem for each equation. Solve.

4. **?** feet – 41 feet = 62 feet

_____

_____

_____

5. 45 inches + **?** inches = 70 inches

_____

_____

_____

Silly Stories

Materials: sharpened pencil, paper clip

To play: Use a paper clip and a sharpened pencil to spin the correct spinner to fill in the blanks for each sentence. Solve the problem. Show your work.

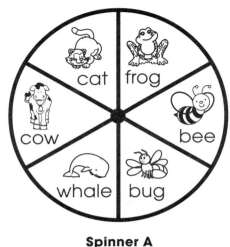

Spinner A   **Spinner B**

1. A _____ drove a jeep _____ feet. A _____
  (A)   (B)   (A)
drove a jeep _____ feet.
  (B)

  Which animal drove the jeep farther? _____

  By how much? _____

2. My brother measured two _____s. One measured
  (A)
  _____ inches and the other measured _____ inches.
  (B)   (B)

  What was the difference in length between the two? _____

3. My _____ is _____ feet tall. It is _____ feet taller
  (A)   (B)   (B)
than my dog.

  How tall would they be together? _____

4. A _____ flew _____ feet through the air. A
  (A)   (B)
_____ flew _____ feet farther through the air.
  (A)   (B)

  How many feet did they fly altogether? _____

Telling and Writing Time

 Essential Question

How are digital and analog clocks used to tell time?
How is time written?

 Warm-Up/Review

Set a timer for 1 minute. Have students see how many times they can touch their toes in that time frame. Then, set the timer for 1 minute again. Have students recite the alphabet as many times as possible in 1 minute. Discuss how 1 minute is equal to 60 seconds.

 Mini-Lesson

Materials: digital clock, analog clock manipulatives

1. Show a digital clock and explain that the hour is shown first and the minutes are shown second. Point out the colon that separates the hours and the minutes. The minutes on a digital clock can be 00–59; the hours on a digital clock can be 1–12. After 12, the hour starts over at 1. Explain that from 12:00 at midnight to 12:00 at noon is called *am* and 12:00 noon to 12:00 at midnight is called *pm*.

2. Show an analog clock. Point out how the large numbers indicate hours, while the smaller lines between numbers show minutes. The numbers are written at each five-minute mark.

3. Explain that the short hand points to the hour and the long hand points to the minute. Demonstrate how it takes the minute hand 5 minutes to move from one number on the clock to the other. Then, skip count by 5s as you move past each number on the clock.

4. Show various times to the nearest 5 minutes on both analog and digital clocks and let students read the time. Then, have students show matching digital and analog clocks.

 Math Talk

Define the term *hands/minutes/hours/clock/time* in your own words.
How are the hour hand and minute hand the same? Different?
What time is it? How do you know?

 Journal Prompt

Draw analog clocks to show the different times in a daily schedule, such as when school starts; start times for lunch, specials, or recess; and when school ends.

Materials

analog clock manipulatives
digital clock
laminated blank number line
dry-erase markers

 Workstations

Activity sheets (pages 131–133)
Time to Fish (page 134)

 Guided Math

⬤ **Remediation: Basic Time Concepts**

1. Write the following times: *1:30, 6:15, 45:11, 7:00*. Read each time aloud. Ask, "Which time is not written correctly?" Review the structure of hours to minutes (hours : minutes). Practice writing and reading digital times.

2. Examine an analog clock together. Begin at 12 and practice moving the minute hand while counting by 5s. Show the top of the hour, quarter after, half past, and quarter till, and the corresponding number and minutes for each location.

3. Point out how the hour hand moves more slowly than the minute hand. Explain that when the hour hand is between hours, it has not made a complete rotation and the smaller of the numbers should be used to name the hour.

4. Say a time aloud and have students draw or show the time on an analog clock and write the matching digital time. Repeat for extra practice.

▢ **On Level: Practicing Reading Clocks**

1. Write a digital time. Ask a student to read the time aloud. Ask, "How do you know which number is the hour and which is the minutes?"

2. Review the concept of am and pm. Brainstorm common activities that take place in the morning, afternoon, evening, and at night. Write example times for each activity.

3. Ask, "How many minutes are in 1 hour?" Practice counting by 5s to 60, pointing to each number on the clock as you count.

4. Model various times and have students count by 5s to determine how many minutes after the hour it is. Model how to count by 5s backward from 12 to tell the number of minutes until the next hour.

5. Have students practice writing various times in words, such as *two thirty* or *six forty-five*.

6. Students should describe to a partner how to tell time to the nearest 5 minutes.

▲ **Enrichment: Elapsed Time**

1. Discuss with students the concept of elapsed time. Ask, "When might we need to know elapsed time?" (Possible answers may include how long a movie lasts or how long a soccer game lasts.)

2. Demonstrate how to count elapsed time by using a number line. Draw a number line marked to 12. Read the following: *It started raining at 2:00. It stopped raining at 5:00. How long did it rain?* Demonstrate starting at the 5 and "hopping" back to 2. Say, "One way to calculate elapsed time is to subtract the hour that something starts from the hour that it ends." (5:00 – 2:00 = 3 hours)

3. Provide more word problems for students to practice calculating elapsed time on their own number lines. Have them write number sentences to show the answers.

4. Demonstrate how to determine elapsed time involving half-past and quarter hour times on the number line. Have students practice elapsed word problems with these times.

 Assess and Extend

Distribute analog clock manipulatives to students. Say times such as *5:30, 10:05,* and *1:15*. Have students show each time on their clocks. Then, have students write the matching digital time.

Telling and Writing Time   ⬤ **Basic Time Concepts**

Look at the time on each digital clock. Write the letter of the matching analog clock.

1. _____

A.

2. _____

B.

3. _____

C.

4. _____

D.

5. _____

E.

6. _____

F.

Name _____   Date _____

 Telling and Writing Time   ☐ Practicing Reading Clocks

Look at each clock. Write the time.

1.

_____

2.

_____

3.

_____

4.

_____

5.

_____

6.

_____

7.

_____

8.

_____

9.

_____

Write each time in words.

10.  _____

11.  _____

12.  _____

Telling and Writing Time   ▲ **Elapsed Time**

Find each amount of time that has passed. Use the clocks for help or draw a number line.

1. The sun came out from behind the clouds at 1:00. It set at 6:00. How long was the sun out?

_____ hours

2. Janet's game started at 2:00. It lasted 1 hour and 40 minutes. What time did the game end?

_____

3. Zoe's favorite movie starts at 7:15. It is 2 hours and 5 minutes long. What time will the movie end?

_____

4. The wind started blowing at 12:00. It stopped at 3:00. How long did the wind blow?

_____ hours

5. It began to rain at 4:30. It stopped raining at 8:30. How long did it rain?

_____ hours

6. A rainbow appeared at 6:00. It disappeared at 8:00. How long did the rainbow last?

_____ hours

Time to Fish

Materials: two colors of counters, 1 die

To play: Each player puts a counter on Start. Players take turns rolling the die and moving that many spaces. If a player lands on a clock, he matches it to a digital time at the bottom and covers the fish with a counter. If none of the times match the clock or the fish is already covered, the player loses a turn. If a player lands on a fishing rod, he can cover the time of his choice. The player to cover the most fish wins.

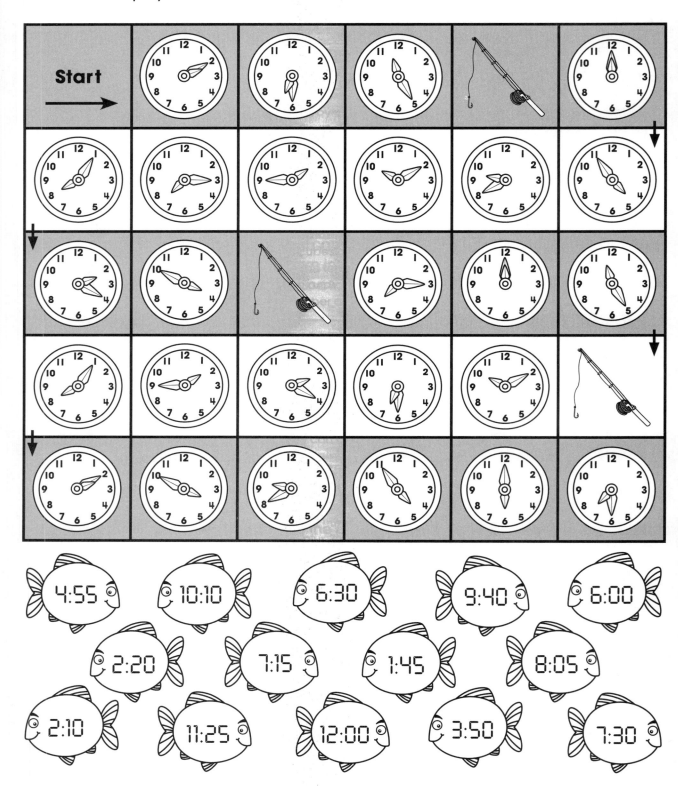

Money

? Essential Question

What strategies can be used to solve money word problems?

C Warm-Up/Review

Create a mind map on the board by writing the word *money* in the center of a large circle. Have volunteers come to the board and write or draw something that comes to mind when they see or hear the word *money*. Then, discuss some of the ideas that were written on the mind map.

★ Mini-Lesson

Materials: coin and bill manipulatives, small prizes to "sell" (such as pencils)

1. Give each group of four students a handful of coins.

2. Have students sort the coins. Ask each group how they chose to sort the coins—for example, by color, size, or value.

3. Discuss the value and unique characteristics of each coin and model how you can count coin values by skip counting. Have each group count their money.

4. Introduce the dollar bill. Examine the bill and explain the symbols on the bill and its value.

5. Offer small items "for sale." For example, offer a pencil for 8¢. Ask each buyer to count the total value of coins aloud. Continue to sell items until each student buys something. Ensure that each student buys only one item and that all coins are collected at the end of the sale.

☐ Math Talk

Why is it important to know the values of coins and bills?

Tell how you count on to find the total amount of money.

Can you make this amount with a different set of coins?

✎ Journal Prompt

Explain how you can use skip counting to find the value of a set of money.

Materials

coin and bill manipulatives
gray and brown paper circles
glue
construction paper
stapler
grocery store advertisements
restaurant menus

 Workstations

Activity sheets (pages 137–139)
Cash Cow (page 140)

 Guided Math

○ **Remediation: Coin Book**

1. Distribute a penny, nickel, dime, and quarter manipulative to each student. Distribute half-dollars and dollars if desired.
2. Have students examine the coins and draw each on two paper circles (one for the front and one for the back).
3. Have students glue their coin drawings to construction paper pages. Help students label pages with coin names and other information, such as values, facts about coin images, unique features, and coin metals.
4. Staple the pages together to make coin books.
5. Skip count aloud five times with each coin value. For example, "1, 2, 3, 4, 5" for pennies and "10, 20, 30, 40, 50" for dimes. Have students write the counting sequences along the bottom of each matching coin page.

□ **On Level: Coin Combinations**

1. Provide coins and have students practice making different values with different coins. Ask, "How can you make 75¢ three different ways? How many pennies are needed to make $1.00? How many dimes?"
2. Have student browse grocery store advertisement flyers and cut out 3–5 items to "purchase." Have students glue the grocery items to construction paper.
3. Instruct students to find the necessary coin and bill combinations to purchase each item, providing guidance if necessary.
4. Have students draw or list the coins and/or bills they used below each item. Challenge students to find at least two different coin and/or bill combinations for each grocery item on their papers.

△ **Enrichment: Money Word Problems**

1. Review the value and name of each coin.
2. Provide a restaurant menu for each pair of students.
3. Instruct each student to order two things from the menu and phrase it to their partner as a word problem. (For example, *I would like to order a hamburger and fries. How much will my total be?*) The partner will add the prices together and present a "bill." Students should check their bills for accuracy.
4. Next, challenge students to order three or more items from the menu at a time and repeat step 3.

 Assess and Extend

Read several money word problems aloud, such as "I have a penny, three nickels, and two quarters. How much money do I have in all?" Students should draw the coins to solve and show their work.

Money

Count each set of coins to find the total value. Write the numbers as you count.

1. (1¢) (1¢) (1¢) (1¢) (1¢) (1¢) (1¢) (1¢) = _____ ¢

___ ___ ___ ___ ___ ___ ___ ___

2. (25¢) (25¢) (25¢) (25¢) = _____ ¢ or $_____ . _____

___ ___ ___ ___

3. (10¢) (10¢) (10¢) (10¢) (10¢) (10¢) (10¢) = _____ ¢

___ ___ ___ ___ ___ ___ ___

4. (5¢) (5¢) (5¢) (5¢) (5¢) (5¢) = _____ ¢

___ ___ ___ ___ ___ ___

5. (5¢) (5¢) (5¢) (5¢) (5¢) (5¢) (5¢) (5¢) = _____ ¢

___ ___ ___ ___ ___ ___ ___ ___

6. (25¢) (25¢) (25¢) (25¢) (25¢) = _____ ¢ or $_____ . _____

___ ___ ___ ___ ___

Name _____ **Date** _____

 **Money** ☐ Coin Combinations

Write how many coins you need to buy each item. Then, write a different combination of coins for the same amount.

1. 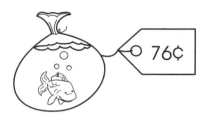 76¢

_____ pennies | _____ pennies
_____ nickels | _____ nickels
_____ dimes | _____ dimes
_____ quarters | _____ quarters

2.  55¢

_____ pennies | _____ pennies
_____ nickels | _____ nickels
_____ dimes | _____ dimes
_____ quarters | _____ quarters

3.  99¢

_____ pennies | _____ pennies
_____ nickels | _____ nickels
_____ dimes | _____ dimes
_____ quarters | _____ quarters

4.  37¢

_____ pennies | _____ pennies
_____ nickels | _____ nickels
_____ dimes | _____ dimes
_____ quarters | _____ quarters

5. 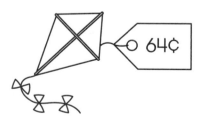 64¢

_____ pennies | _____ pennies
_____ nickels | _____ nickels
_____ dimes | _____ dimes
_____ quarters | _____ quarters

6. 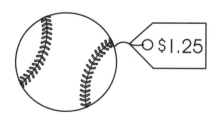 $1.25

_____ pennies | _____ pennies
_____ nickels | _____ nickels
_____ dimes | _____ dimes
_____ quarters | _____ quarters

 **Money**   ▲ Money Word Problems

Use information from the menu to solve each problem. Read each story carefully and decide if it makes sense to add or subtract.

Smokey Joe's Barbecue

MAIN DISHES		SIDE DISHES		BEVERAGES	
Eye-Watering Ham	$3.50	Flame Fries	$1.10	Cola	$0.75
Burning-Hot Ribs	$3.75	Sizzlin' Salad	$1.05	Lemonade	$0.85
Rockin' Roast Beef	$4.25	Tasty Potato Tots	$0.95	Milk	$0.95

1. Maria ordered tots and milk. How much will her lunch cost?

_____

2. Michael ordered roast beef. He paid with a five-dollar bill. How much change will he get?

_____

3. Sam has $4.08. He buys ham as a main dish. How much money does Sam have left?

_____

4. Terone wonders, "How much does an order of ham, fries, and a cola cost?"

_____

5. How much more does roast beef cost than cola?

_____

6. Ryan spent $5.55 for lunch. He got $0.45 back as change. How much money did Ryan start out with?

_____

7. Taylor orders the least expensive item from each section of the menu. How much does she spend?

_____

8. Tracy buys milk for herself and three friends. How much does she spend?

_____

Cash Cow

Materials: coin manipulatives, paper bag

To play: For each round, place the coins in a paper bag. Player 1 will draw a few coins. Player 2 will count the coins and write the total in the first box. Place the coins back into the bag. Repeat two more times, switching players each time. The last player should total all three amounts and write the sum.

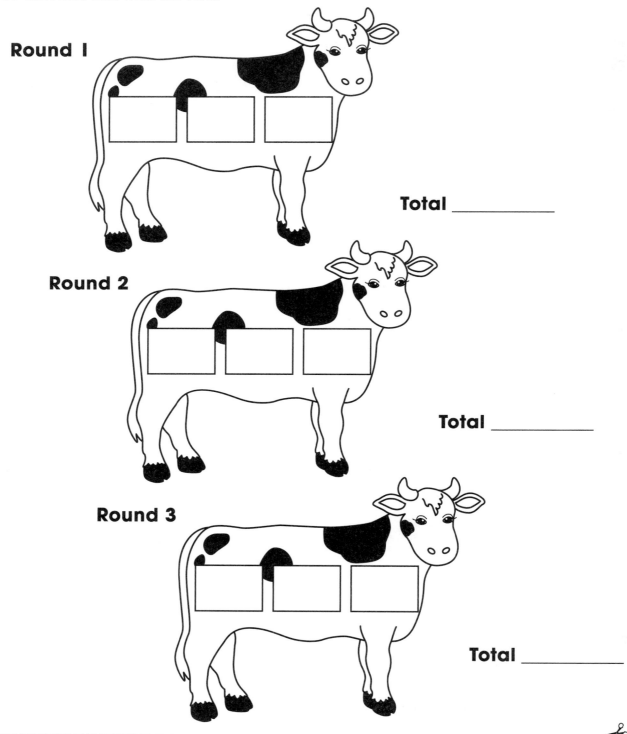

Round 1

Total _____

Round 2

Total _____

Round 3

Total _____

To prep: To differentiate for different levels of students, place different coins and different amounts in the bags. That way, students will be adding amounts appropriate to their level of understanding. Cut off these directions before copying.

Essential Question

How can data be collected and recorded?

 Warm-Up/Review

Pose the following scenario: "Mario and Lynn are going to sell lemonade at their lemonade stand this Friday, Saturday, and Sunday. How can they keep track of their sales each day?" Discuss students' answers.

 Mini-Lesson

1. Define and discuss the terms *data*, *table*, *tally*, and *survey*. Explain that a survey is a way to gather information on a topic. The answers from the survey are the data, or information gathered. The data can be represented by tally marks, or tallies, in a table. Demonstrate how to draw 4 straight marks with a diagonal line across them to represent *5*.

2. Draw a table on the board. Ask, "What kinds of pets do you have at home?" Decide together what the categories will be (for example, *dog, cat, other, no pets*). Ask, "Why do we need to provide categories to choose from? What happens to our results if we don't give a few choices?"

3. Label the table columns with headers (*Pet Type, Tally Marks, Total Number*). Have students come to the board and draw tally marks in the columns to represent their answers. Explain that the tallies are an easy way to quickly count as you go and to find the total number later.

4. Demonstrate how to count the tallies and record the total number for each pet in the table. Discuss the results of the survey together. Ask questions such as, "How many more students liked _____ than _____?" or "How many students were surveyed in all?"

 Math Talk

What is a survey?
Why is the data collected important?
What might happen if the data is not correct?

 Journal Prompt

Your teacher has asked you to take a class survey. What question will you ask? Why? Describe how you will collect and organize the data.

Materials

different colors of counters
jar of pennies, nickels, dimes, and
quarters (manipulatives, if desired)

 Workstations

Activity sheets (pages 143–145)
Sweet Surveys (page 146)

 Guided Math

⭕ Remediation: Organizing Data

1. Gather a large pile of three different colors of counters. Draw a table with the column headers *Color*, *Tally Marks*, and *Total Number*. Under *Color*, write the names of the counter colors.
2. Explain that tables organize information so it is easy to understand quickly. This table will show the number of each color of counters. Have students sort the counters by color. Model how to draw a tally mark in the middle column for each counter.
3. Show how the data is organized by rows. Explain that each tally mark stands for 1 counter. Point out how the tallies are grouped by 5s for easier counting. Write the total number of tallies for each color in the last column.
4. Ask, "Which color had the most counters? Which color had the fewest counters? What is the purpose of using tallies? Why did we also write the total number?"

🔲 On Level: Reading Tables

1. Draw a table with the column headers *Birthday Month* and *Number of Students*. Under *Birthday Month*, write answer choices *March*, *April*, *May*, and *June*. Write 7 tallies for *March*, 2 for *April*, 11 for *May*, and 5 for *June*.
2. Ask, "How can I tell what kind of data the table holds and what it means?" Point out the column headers and row categories.
3. Have volunteers count the tally marks and write the total number of students for each month in the table. Emphasize that all of the data in each row goes together. Ask, "How could I find the total number of birthdays in March and May? What can I do to find how many more students had a birthday in June than in April?"
4. Have each student write two questions about the data and find the corresponding answers.

🔺 Enrichment: Creating Tables

1. Present a jar of mixed coins. Tell students to create a table to record the different types of coins in the jar. Ask, "What column headers will you need? What categories will you have? What title will you use?"
2. Help students draw the table. Include a column for tallies. Have students sort the coins by denomination. Mark a tally for each coin sorted. Ask, "How does writing the tallies in groups of fives help you organize the information?" Direct students to write the total number of each coin in the table.
3. Examine the data together. Ask, "How many pennies and dimes are there in all? How many more quarters than nickels are there? Using the table, how can I find the total number of coins in the container?" Discuss how word clues such as *in all* or *how many more* signal which operation to use.
4. Have students write three questions about the data and find the corresponding answers.

 Assess and Extend

Write the following problem on the board: *Mario and Lynn sold 8 glasses of lemonade on Friday, 9 glasses of lemonade on Saturday, and 11 glasses of lemonade on Sunday at their lemonade stand.* Have students create a table with tally marks and totals to display the data.

Collecting and Recording Data   ● Organizing Data

Colin took a survey of his classmates' favorite fruits and sports. Record the data in each table.

Fruit	Tally Marks	Total Number
🍎		
🍌		
🍐		
🍍		

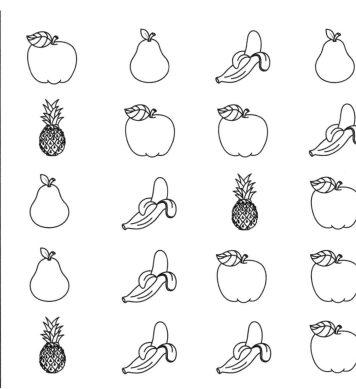

Sport	Tally Marks	Total Number
🏀		
⚾		
🏈		
⚽		

🔲 Collecting and Recording Data   ⬛ Reading Tables

Read each paragraph. Record the data in the table. Use the table to answer the question.

1. Grace sells T-shirts. On Monday, she sold 3 large and 4 medium shirts. On Tuesday, she sold 5 small and 2 large shirts. On Thursday, she sold 1 medium and 4 large shirts. She sold 3 small and 2 large shirts on Friday.

T-shirt Size	Tally Marks	Total Number

How many large T-shirts did Grace sell this week? _____

2. Jacob plays on a traveling hockey team. In August, his team won 6 games and lost 3 games. In September, they tied 2 games and won 5 games. In October, the team won 4 games and lost 2 games. They lost 3 games and won 3 games in December.

Game Outcome	Tally Marks	Total Number

By winter break, had the team won or lost more games?

_____

3. In classroom A, 8 students ride the bus to school and 4 students arrive by car. In classroom B, 3 students walk and 9 others ride the bus. In classroom C, 2 students arrive by car, 7 ride the bus, and 3 walk.

Travel Method	Tally Marks	Total Number

How many students ride the bus? _____

Collecting and Recording Data ▲ Creating Tables

Write three questions with answer choices to ask your classmates. Perform the surveys or create your own data. Record the data in the tables.

Question: _____

_____

Answer Choices	Tally Marks	Total

Question: _____

_____

Answer Choices	Tally Marks	Total

Question: _____

_____

Answer Choices	Tally Marks	Total

Sweet Surveys

Materials: sharpened pencil, paper clip

To play: For each round, use the sharpened pencil and paper clip to spin the spinner and gather data. Spin 10 times. Using tally marks, record the data for each spin in the table. Write the final total for each category.

Round 1

Candy	Tally Marks	Totals
gum		
chocolate		
mint		

Round 2

Dessert	Tally Marks	Totals
cake		
ice cream		
cupcake		

Round 3

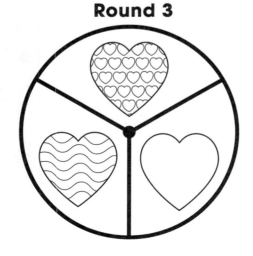

Heart	Tally Marks	Totals
plain		
mini hearts		
striped		

Line Plots

 Essential Question

How is a line plot used to display and analyze measurement data?

Warm-Up/Review

Distribute laminated blank number lines and dry-erase markers to students. On the board, model numbering a number line from 0 to 10, then 5 to 15. Have students practice numbering their number lines various ways, such as to 50 by 5s, or from 10 to 100 by 10s.

 Mini-Lesson

Materials: sticky notes

1. Define a line plot as a type of graph that uses a number line with Xs to show pieces of data. Point out the main parts of a line plot (number line, title, axis label, and data points).

2. Have each student remove a shoe to find her shoe size. Point out that some shoe sizes come in half sizes and model how to write a half shoe size. Have them record the shoe sizes on their sticky notes. Have students randomly place their sticky notes on the board.

3. Explain, "A line plot would be a good way to show the shoe sizes of the students in our class because our data is numbers, not categories, and we want to show frequency, or how often a shoe size (data point) occurs." Draw a blank line plot on the board. Say, "First, we determine what section of the number line best fits the data. We can look at the lowest and highest shoe sizes and use those as our boundaries for numbering the number line."

4. Guide students to use the highest and lowest shoe sizes and complete the number line. Add a title and label the axis. Explain that amounts that do not have any data still need to be shown so the number line is unbroken.

5. Have students choose a sticky note from the board and add it to the line plot in the proper place on the number line. Then, replace each one with an *X*. Ask questions such as, "Which shoe size occurs the most? The least? How many students have shoe sizes larger than __?" etc.

6. Discuss other measurements that could be plotted on a number line, such as plant heights.

 Math Talk

What do the Xs on a line plot represent?
Tell how to read a line plot.
Explain how you know you have plotted all of the data.

 Journal Prompt

Can we leave out a number on the number line when plotting data? Why or why not?

Materials

colored linking cubes
blank laminated line plots
dry-erase markers
rulers
paper strips
scissors

 Workstations

Activity sheets (pages 149–151)
How Does Your Garden Grow?
(page 152)
Sweet Surveys (page 146)

 Guided Math

⭕ **Remediation: Concrete Line Plots**

1. Give each student a random assortment of colored linking cubes and a blank line plot. Have students sort the cubes, link them by color, and place the stacks in order from shortest to longest. Then, guide students to place each stack in order by length on the line plot, placing the stacks horizontally so they clearly show frequency.

2. Say, "Using the actual objects makes the line plot more difficult to read. So, mathematicians use an *X* to represent each object. But, we need to know what the *X* represents, so first we need to count the number of linking cubes in each stack and label the line plot." Count the number of linking cubes in each stack and label the line plot. Then, write an *X* for each stack of linking cubes above each label.

3. Point out the marks on a ruler and explain how a ruler is like a number line. When plotting items by length, students can use the ruler to help create a line plot.

4. Repeat steps 1 and 2 with a new set of linking cubes. Encourage students to use the ruler and skip making the concrete line plot step when they are ready.

🔲 **On Level: Creating and Interpreting Line Plots**

1. Gather a large assortment of linking cubes. Link them by color and place the stacks in order from shortest to longest. Measure the length of each stack and record the measurements. Model creating a line plot to show your data. Point out the highest and lowest numbers, mark them, and mark the measurements in between. Then, plot your data.

2. Distribute laminated blank line plots to students. Distribute a random assortment of linking cubes to each student. Have them repeat the activity to create their own data and line plots.

3. Students should use the line plots to answer the following questions: *Which length was most common? Least common? How many stacks measured longer than 2 inches? Which length occurred only twice?* etc. Have students use their line plots to justify their answers.

🔺 **Enrichment: Working with Data**

1. Have each student measure 3 crayons in their desk to the nearest inch. Pool the students' data and have each student use the data to create a line plot, with guidance as necessary.

2. Ask, "How many crayons did we measure in all?" Model counting all of the *X*s to find the answer. Model finding the answer to the following question: *What is the difference between the shortest and longest crayons we measured?*

3. Give each student a paper strip and scissors. Have students cut their strips into 10 pieces of varying lengths. Then, have students measure their strips to the nearest inch and plot the data on a line plot. Finally, have students use their line plots to answer questions such as *Did any strips have the same measurement? If so, how many?*

 Assess and Extend

Have students measure the widths of six books in their desks to the nearest inch. Then, have them create a line plot to show the data and write a true statement about the data.

Line Plots   ● Concrete Line Plots

The line plot shows the height in feet of the sunflowers in Ms. Bailey's garden. Read the graph and answer the questions.

Sunflower Height (ft.)

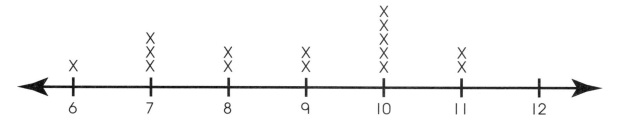

1. How many sunflowers are 10 feet tall?

_____

2. How many sunflowers are 11 feet tall?

_____

3. Which height shows three sunflowers?

_____

4. Which height shows the least amount of sunflowers?

_____

5. Ms. Bailey measured two more sunflowers. The first one was 9 feet tall and the second one was 6 feet tall. Mark Xs on the line plot to add the sunflowers to the graph.

Line Plots   Creating and Interpreting Line Plots

Lin made necklaces of different lengths to sell at a fund-raiser. Use the data to complete the line plot. Answer the questions.

Lengths of Necklaces

17 in.	19 in.
21 in.	18 in.
17 in.	17 in.
18 in.	20 in.
19 in.	15 in.

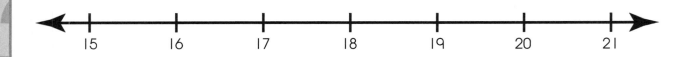

15   16   17   18   19   20   21

1. What was the total number of 15-inch necklaces?

_____

2. What was the total number of 18-inch necklaces?

_____

3. Lin made one more necklace that was 20 inches long. Graph that necklace on the line plot.

_____

4. What was the total number of necklaces that Lin made?

_____

 **Line Plots**   ▲ Working with Data

Mr. Walker's class planted beans. After a week, the class recorded the heights of the sprouts. Use the data to make a line plot. Answer the questions.

Bean Sprouts

Height	Number
4 cm	4
5 cm	7
6 cm	4
7 cm	6
8 cm	3

I. Which two heights had the same number of bean sprouts?

_____

2. How many bean sprouts were 7 centimeters in height?

_____

3. What was the total number of bean sprouts?

_____

4. How many more bean sprouts were 5 centimeters than 4 centimeters in height?

_____

How Does Your Garden Grow?

Materials: one-inch square graph paper

To play: Each partner chooses a task card. Use the graph paper to record the data from the card on a line plot. Write a question from the line plot for each partner to answer. Partners should check each other's line plots for accuracy. Repeat with other cards.

Heights of Tomato Plants

25 in.	28 in.	26 in.
26 in.	26 in.	26 in.
25 in.	28 in.	27 in.
27 in.	29 in.	27 in.
27 in.	29 in.	28 in.

Heights of Sunflowers

4 ft.	7 ft.	3 ft.
6 ft.	6 ft.	6 ft.
6 ft.	4 ft.	6 ft.
5 ft.	5 ft.	7 ft.
4 ft.	5 ft.	4 ft.

Heights of Bean Plants

10 cm	9 cm	10 cm
8 cm	7 cm	10 cm
8 cm	9 cm	7 cm
10 cm	8 cm	9 cm
10 cm	6 cm	10 cm

Heights of Corn Stalks

55 in.	59 in.	55 in.
54 in.	59 in.	55 in.
59 in.	59 in.	56 in.
57 in.	53 in.	55 in.
55 in.	55 in.	54 in.

Heights of Daisies

15 cm	16 cm	16 cm
15 cm	16 cm	19 cm
17 cm	17 cm	20 cm
17 cm	18 cm	17 cm
18 cm	19 cm	15 cm

Heights of Garden Statues

3 ft.	3 ft.	3 ft.
4 ft.	4 ft.	1 ft.
2 ft.	5 ft.	2 ft.
1 ft.	1 ft.	2 ft.
2 ft.	2 ft.	3 ft.

To prep: Copy on card stock for durability. If desired, laminate. Cut apart the task cards and place in a center with the directions.

Picture Graphs

 Essential Question

How are picture graphs used to display and analyze data?

 Warm-Up/Review

Pose the following question: "What is your favorite type of pizza?" Each student should select three choices, such as *pepperoni*, *cheese*, or *veggie* and survey classmates using tally marks to collect and record the data. Discuss students' results.

Note: Save the results for the Assess activity.

 Mini-Lesson

1. Define *picture graph*. Explain that these kinds of graphs display information in a similar way to bar graphs. Instead of bars, a picture is used to represent for an amount. Explain that picture graphs have a key that tells the amount each picture represents.

2. Draw a picture graph on the board. (Explain each part of the graph as you draw it.) Label the graph *Trading Cards*. Create 4 rows and write the names *Chase*, *Taylor*, *Jose*, and *Isabelle* along the left side of the graph. Include a key that shows that 1 circle means 1 trading card. Draw 6 circles in the row for Chase, 4 for Taylor, 5 for Jose, and 7 for Isabelle.

3. Ask, "How many trading cards does Chase have? Does Taylor have more or less trading cards than Jose? Can you tell without counting? Which student has 4 trading cards? Which student has the most trading cards? How many total trading cards does this group have?" Emphasize vocabulary like *most*, *more than*, and *total*.

4. Adjust the key to 1 circle equals 2 trading cards on the *Trading Cards* picture graph. Erase the circles. Explain that now each circle will represent 2 trading cards. Draw 3 circles for Chase, 2 circles for Taylor, 2 and a half circles for Jose, and 3 and a half circles for Isabelle. Ask students, "Why did I draw half circles for Jose and Isabelle?" Explain the concept of half symbols used in picture graphs.

 Math Talk

How does a key affect the way a picture graph looks?
Why is the title important?
Compare and contrast a picture graph with a bar graph.

 Journal Prompt

Draw a blank picture graph. Label the parts.

Materials

counters

 Workstations

Activity sheets (pages 155–157)
Spin-a-Graph (page 158)

 Guided Math

⬤ **Remediation: Reading Picture Graphs**

1. Draw a picture graph. Title the graph *Tickets Won*, and draw a key indicating each counter means 1 ticket. Label the rows *Cory*, *Grace*, *Owen*, and *Felipe*.

2. Have students place 5 counters on the row for Cory, 3 for Grace, 6 for Owen, and 4 for Felipe. Point out the key. Reinforce that each counter represents 1 ticket. Counters should not touch each other so that they are recognized as 1 unit each. They should also be aligned in columns as well as rows to make it easier to compare rows.

3. Ask, "How many tickets does Grace have? What did you do to find your answer? Does any other student have 3 tickets? Which student has 4 tickets? How many students have more than 4 tickets? Who has the most tickets? How do you know without counting?"

4. Model how to write a summary sentence about the picture graph.

◼ **On Level: Analyzing Picture Graphs**

1. Draw a table titled *Points Scored in Soccer*. Include rows labeled for the following players and the number of points scored: *Chloe* (4), *Hannah* (3), *Miguel* (2), and *Wyatt* (4).

2. Draw a picture graph and include a key that shows 1 circle equals 2 points scored. Have volunteers use the information in the table to draw the correct number of circles next to each student.

3. Ask, "Which student scored the most points this season? How do you know? Who scored 4 points? How did you find your answer? Which two students scored 8 points? Who scored more points— Hannah or Wyatt? How many more? Why is the key important for the graph?"

4. Have students write two questions about the data and have a partner answer the questions.

▲ **Enrichment: Interpreting Picture Graphs**

1. Draw a picture graph titled *Fall Birthdays* and include a key indicating each cake represents 2 students. Label the rows *September*, *October*, *November*, and *December*.

2. Say, "Three students have a birthday in September. How can I show that on the picture graph?" Draw 1 cake and half of another. Explain that each cake means 2 students, so half of a cake means 1 student.

3. Say, "In October, there are 5 more birthdays than in September. What do I do to find the total number of birthdays in October? How do I show that on the picture graph?" Have students draw the correct number of cakes on the picture graph. (4 cakes)

4. Ask, "Why is the key important for the graph? How would the data change if each cake represented 1 student? How does increasing the number of students represented by each cake change the picture graph?"

5. Have students write three questions about the data and have a partner answer them.

 Assess and Extend

Students should use the data collected during the warm-up to create a picture graph.

Picture Graphs   ● Reading Picture Graphs

Look at the graph. Answer the questions.

Free Throw Contest

Caden

Ethan

Olivia

Trisha

 = 1 basket made

1. What does each basketball in the graph mean? _____

2. Which student made the most baskets? _____

3. How many baskets did Ethan make? _____

4. Which student made 4 baskets? _____

5. How many baskets did Olivia and Caden make in all? _____

6. How many more baskets did Trisha make than Olivia? _____

Picture Graphs   Analyzing Picture Graphs

Look at the graph. Answer the questions.

Tomato Seeds Planted

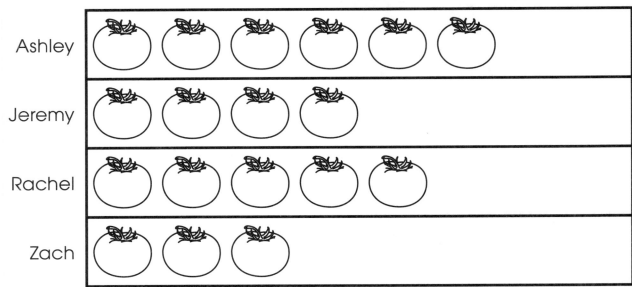

 = 2 tomato seeds

1. Which student planted the most seeds? _____

2. How many seeds did Rachel plant? _____

3. Who planted more seeds—Jeremy or Zach? _____

4. Which student planted 6 tomato seeds? _____

5. How many more seeds did Ashley plant than Jeremy? _____

6. How many seeds did Jeremy and Rachel plant together? _____

7. How many more seeds did Ashley and Rachel plant than Jeremy and Zach? _____

8. What is the total number of seeds planted by this group of students? _____

Name _____   Date _____

Look at the graph. Answer the questions.

Books Henry Read This Month

 = 2 books

1. Which kind of book did Henry read the most? _____

2. How many biographies did Henry read? _____

3. How many more mystery books did he read than
biographies? _____

4. Which kind of book did Henry read 7 of? _____

5. How many more fiction and sports books did he read than
mysteries? _____

6. What is the total number of books Henry read this month? _____

7. How would the amounts change if each picture in the pictograph
represented 1 book instead of 2 books read? _____

_____

Spin-a-Graph

Materials: sharpened pencil, paper clip, scrap paper

To play: For each round, use the sharpened pencil and paper clip to spin the spinner. Use the key to record each spin in the correct column. (It may be helpful to record tallies on scrap paper first.) After 10 spins, end the round and add the totals. In Round 1, the first player will write a question and the second player will answer. In Round 2, the second player will write a question and the first player will answer it. Be sure to check the key for each round.

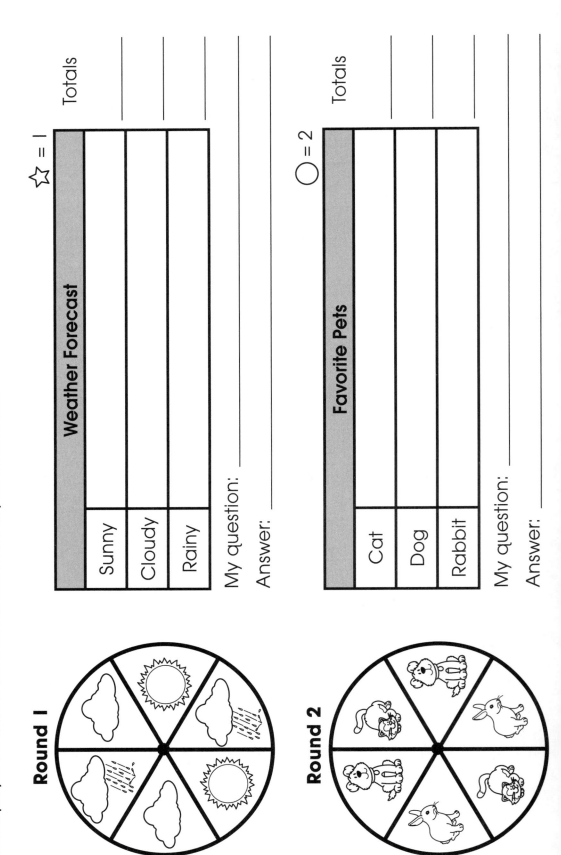

Round 1

☆ = 1

Weather Forecast	Totals
Sunny	
Cloudy	
Rainy	

My question: _____

Answer: _____

Round 2

◯ = 2

Favorite Pets	Totals
Cat	
Dog	
Rabbit	

My question: _____

Answer: _____

Bar Graphs

 Essential Question

How are bar graphs used to display and analyze data?

Warm-Up/Review

Review the different types of graphs the class has studied. Draw an example of each graph on the board. Discuss the parts of each graph and have volunteers label each part. As a class, discuss how the graphs are alike and how they are different.

 Mini-Lesson

Materials: colored construction paper, sticky notes

1. Review the term *graph*. Remind students that a graph shows information. Explain that in a bar graph, the height of each bar stands for an amount.

2. Ask students to take a sheet of construction paper that represents their favorite color. Build a whole-class bar graph on a classroom wall. Help students organize their papers in groups by color. Reinforce that the sheets of paper cannot overlap or have gaps in between them.

3. Label the vertical axis with numbers and the horizontal axis with color names written on sticky notes. Model how to read the graph when all students have posted their papers on the wall. Demonstrate how to follow the top of each color bar to the number on the left.

4. Model how to compare the heights of the bars. Ask, "Which favorite color is the most common? How many students like yellow? Do more students like blue or green? How many more?" Use vocabulary like *most*, *more than*, and *total*.

 Math Talk

What are graphs used for? Why are they important?

Compare and contrast a bar graph with a line plot/picture graph.

Explain how you know that number is the greatest/least.

 Journal Prompt

Tell why a graph helps you see data better than a chart or a list.

Materials

colored linking cubes

Workstations

Activity sheets (pages 161–163)
Tic-Tac-Toe Graphing (page 164)

Guided Math

Remediation: Creating Bar Graphs

1. Collect 20 multicolored cubes. Have students sort and stack the cubes by color. Arrange each stack to look like a bar on a bar graph.
2. Draw a bar graph. Write the name of each cube color along the bottom. Have students arrange their stacks correctly on the graph.
3. Write numbers along the left side of the graph to match the height of a cube. Discuss how the numbers start at 0 and go up by 1 like a number line.
4. Model how to compare the stacks. Ask, "Which color has the tallest bar? Which color has the shortest bar? What does that mean?" Explain that the taller the bar, the larger the number.
5. Practice relating the bar and its height to the amount of each color. Ask, "Which color has 4 cubes? How many cubes are red? How many blue and red cubes are there?"

On Level: Reading Bar Graphs

1. Draw the two axes of a bar graph on the board. Title the graph *After-School Activities*. Label the categories on the *x*-axis *Art*, *Computer*, *Music*, and *Sports*. Write a scale in increments of 2 on the *y*-axis.
2. Draw bars to represent the number of students who reported their favorite after-school activity: art (3), computer (6), music (4), and sports (9). Model how to follow the top of a bar to the number of students.
3. Interpret the data together. Ask, "What does it mean when the top of a bar falls between two lines on the scale? How many students are involved in each activity? How do I find out how many more students play sports than create art? How do I find the number of students who use the computer or take a music class after school? How would I find the total number of students who reported their favorite activity?"
4. Have students write three facts that the graph shows.

Enrichment: Analyzing Bar Graphs

1. Draw a double bar graph titled *Summer Soccer Program*. Draw a scale with intervals of 2 and write three labels on the *x*-axis for years (*2015*, *2016*, and *2017*). Draw two bars for each year: 2015 boys (12) and girls (5), 2016 boys (10) and girls (8), and 2017 boys (9) and girls (12). Shade the bars for girls in each year.
2. Draw a key and explain how to tell the two groups of data apart on the bar graph. Ask, "Why is one bar shaded for each year? How many years are shown on the graph? What information does the graph show?"
3. Discuss how to interpret the information. Ask, "In 2016, how can you find the total number of girls and boys who participated in the summer soccer program? How can you find how many more boys played soccer in 2015 than in 2017? In which year did more girls than boys participate in the soccer program?"
4. Have students write questions about the data and have partners answer them.

Assess and Extend

Have students draw a blank bar graph and label its parts. Then, challenge students to think of a survey question and four choices. Students should survey their classmates and then complete their blank graphs with the information.

Name _____   Date _____

Look at the table. Create a bar graph from the data. Then, answer the questions.

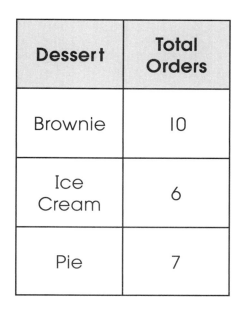

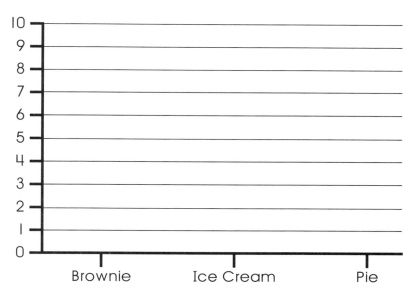

Dessert Orders

Dessert	Total Orders
Brownie	10
Ice Cream	6
Pie	7

1. How many customers ordered a piece of pie? _____

2. Which dessert was ordered the most? _____

3. Which dessert was ordered the least? _____

4. How many more customers ordered a brownie
than ice cream? _____

5. How many total customers ordered ice cream
or pie? _____

6. How many customers ordered a dessert in all? _____

Name_____   Date _____

Look at the graph. Answer the questions.

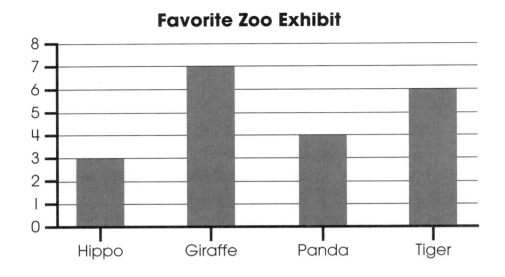

Favorite Zoo Exhibit

1. Which exhibit got the most votes? _____

2. How many students voted for the exhibit with the
   most votes? _____

3. What does it mean when the bar is between two numbers on
   the scale?

   _____

   _____

4. How can you tell which exhibit was more popular—the panda or
   the tiger?

   _____

   _____

5. How many more students liked the giraffe exhibit than the hippo
   exhibit? _____

6. How many students liked the giraffe and tiger exhibits
   in all?_____

Bar Graphs   ▲ Analyzing Bar Graphs

Look at the graph. Answer the questions.

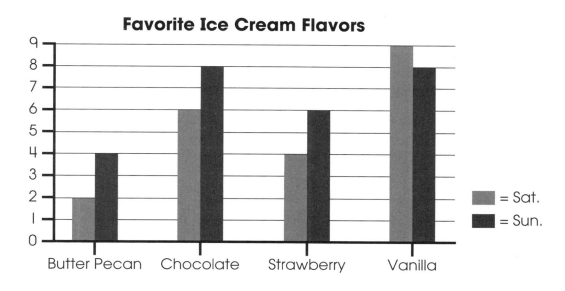

Favorite Ice Cream Flavors

1. Which flavor was most popular on Saturday? _____

2. How many customers ordered that flavor on Saturday? _____

3. How many total customers ordered strawberry ice cream this weekend? _____

4. On Sunday, how many more customers ordered vanilla than butter pecan? _____

5. How many customers ordered the two most popular flavors on Saturday? _____

6. How can you tell which flavor was the least favorite this weekend?

   _____

   _____

7. How many total customers were served on Saturday? _____

8. How many more total customers were served on Sunday than Saturday? _____

Tic-Tac-Toe Graphing

Materials: two colors of counters

To play: Choose a question on the board. Use the graph to answer it. If the player is correct, she places her counter on the question. If she is not correct, she loses a turn. The first person to cover three spaces in a row wins.

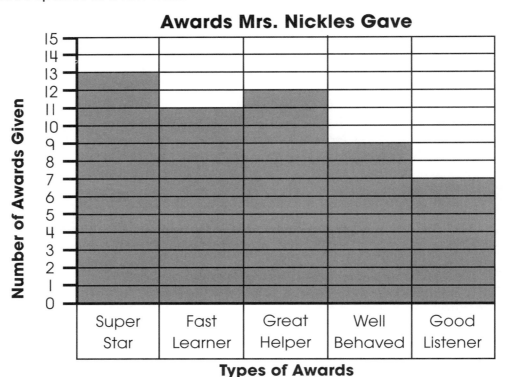

Awards Mrs. Nickles Gave

Which award was given to 11 students?	Which two awards were given to 23 students in all?	How many more Super Star awards than Fast Learner awards were given?
A	**B**	**C**
How many Super Star and Well Behaved awards were given altogether?	Which two awards were given to 20 students in all?	Which award was given out the least?
D	**E**	**F**
How many Great Helper awards were given?	Which award was given out to 7 students?	How many more Great Helper awards were given out than Good Listener awards?
G	**H**	**I**

Identifying Polygons

 ? Essential Question

Why is it important to know the attributes of two-dimensional shapes?

C Warm-Up/Review

Brainstorm examples of plane shapes in students' environments. Ask them to think about the classroom, school, playground, and home. List the examples on the board.

 ★ Mini-Lesson

Materials: pattern blocks, tangrams, and other shape cut outs

1. Draw and label the following polygons on the board: square, rectangle, triangle, hexagon, pentagon, rhombus, trapezoid, and parallelogram. Point out the attributes of each shape. Introduce the vocabulary terms *polygon*, *side*, *angle*, and *vertex*.

2. Compare and contrast the polygons. Ask, "Which shape has 3 straight sides? How many sides does a hexagon have? How many vertices does a square have?"

3. Use pattern blocks, tangrams, and shape cut outs to reinforce shape names and attributes. Move the pattern blocks in different positions so that students recognize shapes in different forms.

4. Have partners create an attributes chart (number of angles, number of sides, etc.) using the hands-on shapes.

 Math Talk

Describe your favorite 2-D shape. What are the attributes of the shape?

Where can you find this shape in the real world?

What happens if I turn this shape? Is it still the same shape? How do you know?

 Journal Prompt

Draw a superhero using only polygons. Label the polygons used in the drawing.

Materials

pattern blocks
tangrams
index cards
dry-erase boards and markers
2 colors of crayons or markers

 Workstations

Activity sheets (pages 167–169)
Bump-a-Shape (page 170)

 Guided Math

Remediation: Identifying Polygons

1. Use pattern blocks to identify and reinforce recognition and details of the shapes from the mini-lesson.
2. Choose a triangle. Ask, "Are the sides of this shape straight or curved? How many sides are there? How many vertices does it have? What is the name of this shape?" Have students find matching triangle tangrams.
3. Follow the same process for vocabulary with descriptions of each shape. Ask, "Which shape has 4 sides and 4 vertices? Which shape has 6 sides? What shape is a stop sign?"
4. Model how to trace a pattern block on a piece of paper. Demonstrate how to reposition it and trace it again so that students learn to recognize the same shapes in different positions. Label each group of shapes with their correct names. Ask, "Does the size of a figure change its basic shape? Does the way the figure is turned or positioned change its basic shape?"
5. Have students list each shape with at least one defining attribute.

On Level: Defining Shape Attributes

1. Have students create a set of flash cards with defining attributes of shapes. Students should write the name of a shape on the front of an index card. Then, list attributes of that shape on the back of the card. For example, *4 equal sides*, *4 vertices* for a *rhombus* card.
2. Have students study their cards and quiz each other.
3. Distribute dry-erase boards and markers to students. Use terms from the cards to give students step-by-step directions to draw shapes. For example, say, "Draw a shape that has 4 sides." Students may not all draw the same shape. Then, give another clue: "This shape has 4 equal sides." Students should change their shapes to reflect the new information. Continue until all of the details are given. Check students' drawings. Repeat the activity with other shapes.

Enrichment: Composing and Decomposing Shapes

1. Compare and contrast all quadrilaterals. Discuss the number and length of sides and whether opposite sides have even lengths. Ask, "How are a rectangle and a parallelogram alike? How are they different? How are trapezoids similar to parallelograms? How are they different?"
2. Use pattern blocks to model how figures can be composed of other basic shapes. For example, a trapezoid can be composed of three triangles, and a rectangle can be composed of two squares.
3. Allow students to trace the outlines of pattern blocks with one color and trace the shapes within the larger figure with a different color. Identify the figure and the shapes within the figure.
4. Have students discuss composing and decomposing figures. Then, have them draw examples of shapes composed of other shapes.

 Assess and Extend

Say various clues to several polygon shapes such as, "I have 3 vertices and 3 sides. What am I? (triangle)" or "I have an odd number of sides (pentagon or triangle). What am I?" For each clue, have students draw the polygon and label it.

Identifying Polygons   ○ Identifying Polygons

Follow the directions to color the shapes.

1. Color the triangles green.

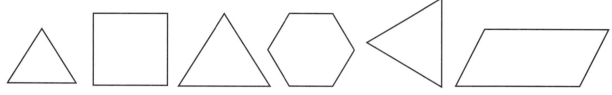

2. Color the hexagons blue.

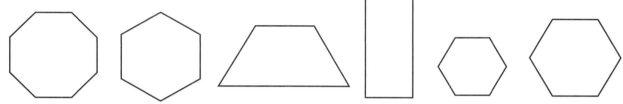

3. Color the trapezoids purple.

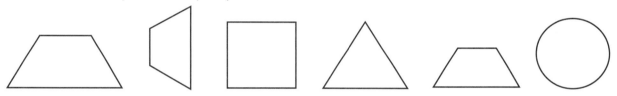

4. Color the octagons red.

5. Color the rectangles yellow.

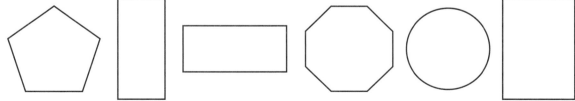

6. Color the circles orange.

Identifying Polygons

Write the letter or letters of each shape described.

A   B   C 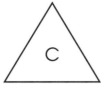 D E

F   G   H   I

1. has four sides _____

2. has six vertices _____

3. has no straight sides _____

4. has more than five sides _____

5. has at least three vertices _____

6. is the shape of a stop sign _____

7. has at least one pair of opposite sides parallel _____

8. all four sides are equal length _____

9. has less than four vertices _____

10. is a two-dimensional shape _____

Identifying Polygons   ▲ Composing and Decomposing Shapes

Identify the figure. Then, draw lines to show what shapes can be used to compose the figure.

1.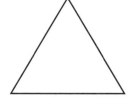

Main figure: _____

Composed of: _____

_____

2.

Main figure: _____

Composed of: _____

_____

3.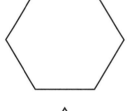

Main figure: _____

Composed of: _____

_____

4.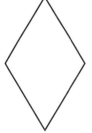

Main figure: _____

Composed of: _____

_____

5.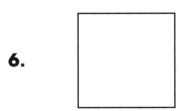

Main figure: _____

Composed of: _____

_____

6.

Main figure: _____

Composed of: _____

_____

Bump-a-Shape

Materials: sharpened pencil, paper clip, 20 counters (10 each of two different colors)

To play: Each player should take 10 counters of the same color. Players take turns. Use the sharpened pencil and paper clip to spin the spinner. Read the name of the shape the spinner lands on. Cover a matching shape with a counter. You may bump the other player off of a shape if the spinner lands on the same shape. The first player to run out of counters wins the game.

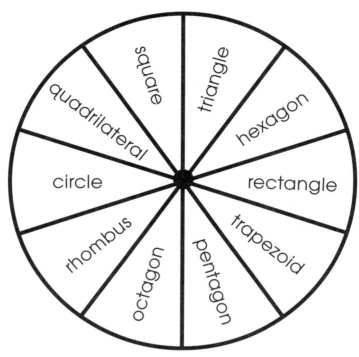

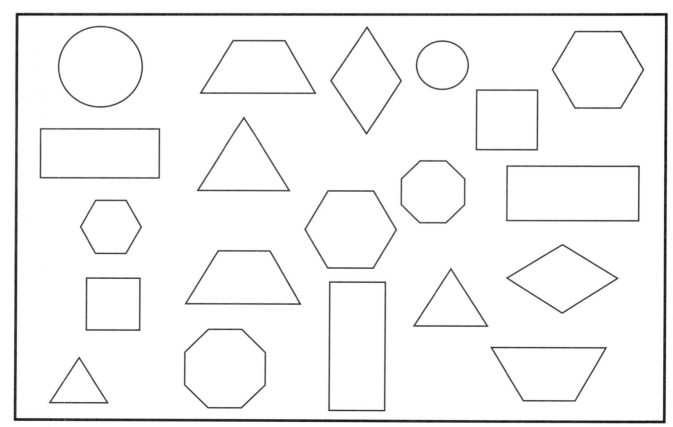

Identifying Solid Figures

 ## Essential Question

Why is it important to know the attributes of three-dimensional shapes?

 ## Warm-Up/Review

Review the difference between 2-D and 3-D shapes. Tell the class that you will say the name of a figure. If it is a plane, or 2-D, figure, they should hold their hand out straight. If it is a solid, or 3-D, figure, they should hold up a fist.

 ## Mini-Lesson

(*Note*: Lessons in this unit use the technical definition which states that edges and faces must be straight, not curved.)

Materials: models of solid shapes

1. Draw a square, rectangle, triangle, and circle on the board. Identify these shapes as two-dimensional, or plane, figures.

2. Show models of a sphere, cone, cylinder, rectangular prism, square pyramid, and cube. Identify these as three-dimensional, or solid, figures. Discuss the similarities and differences between the 2-D and 3-D shapes.

3. Compare and contrast the solids. Describe the attributes of each shape using the terms *edge*, *face*, and *vertex*.

4. Show each figure and identify each of its faces. Emphasize that solid figures can have differently shaped faces on the same solid. Hold the solid from each angle to focus on one face at a time. Determine which solids have curved sides by testing to see which ones roll.

5. Point out the number of vertices, touching each one as you count. Run your finger along each edge to identify where 2 faces of the solid meet.

6. With partners, have students draw and label real-world solid shapes.

 ## Math Talk

Describe your favorite 3-D shape. What are the attributes of the shape?

Where can you find this shape in the real world?

Define the terms *face*, *edge*, and *vertex* in your own words.

 ## Journal Prompt

What makes a solid shape different from a plane shape? What makes them the same? Draw a Venn diagram to compare and contrast the two types of shapes.

Materials

various solid figures
paper bag

 Workstations

Activity sheets (pages 173–175)
Roll Four-in-a-Row (page 176)

 Guided Math

⬤ **Remediation: Recognizing Faces on Solids**

1. Focus on the faces of a solid. Model how to place a solid face down on a piece of paper and trace it. Do this for each face. Examine the shapes.
2. Ask, "How many faces does this solid have? Are all of the faces the same shape? What is the name of each shape?" Follow the same process and make a list of the face shapes found on each solid.
3. Reinforce that a face is a flat surface. Some solids have a curved surface (cylinder, cone, sphere). Test whether each solid can roll smoothly to identify curved surfaces.
4. Place three solids in a group. Ask comparing and contrasting questions such as, "Which shape has two circular faces? Which shape has six square faces? Which shape has no faces?"
5. Have partners choose two solids to compare using the correct vocabulary.

◼ **On Level: Classifying Solids**

1. Focus on the terms used to describe and classify solids (*face, edge, vertex*). Examine and identify each face of the solids together. Count the number of edges and vertices.
2. Compare and contrast the solids. Reinforce math vocabulary with descriptions of each shape. Ask, "How are a cone and a cylinder alike? Different? Which solids can roll and why? How are a square pyramid and triangular prism alike? Different?"
3. Practice sorting the solids by given criteria. Ask, "Which solids have a triangular face? Which solids have a square face? Which solids have a circular face? Which solids have 5 or more vertices? Which solid is unlike the rest? How is it different? Which solids have more than 8 edges?"
4. Have each student choose a solid and identify it by the number of faces, edges, and vertices.

▲ **Enrichment: Differentiating Solids**

1. Have students hold each solid. Direct them to touch and identify each face shape. Encourage them to run their fingers along each edge and touch each vertex as they count the attributes of each solid.
2. Place the solids in a paper bag. Let students take turns closing their eyes, choosing a shape, and trying to identify it just by touch.
3. After each student has had a turn, instruct students to write riddles for each solid using the appropriate vocabulary. For example, "I am similar to a cube, but my edges may not all be equal lengths."
4. Let students practice solving each other's riddles.
5. Challenge students to select one solid and write a commercial with selling points for the figure.

 Assess and Extend

Have students answer the prompt: *How can you tell the difference between a plane shape and a solid shape?* Students should draw shapes or use words to explain their reasoning.

Identifying Solid Figures   Recognizing Faces on Solids

Follow the directions to color each solid. Write the name on the line.

Solid Names		
cone	cube	cylinder
rectangular prism	sphere	triangular pyramid

1. Color the solid that has two circular faces.

   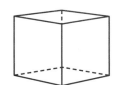

Solid: _____

2. Color the solid that has no faces.

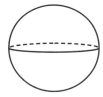   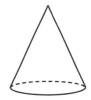   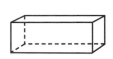

Solid: _____

3. Color the solid that has at least four rectangular faces.

   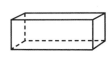

Solid: _____

4. Color the solid that has four triangular faces.

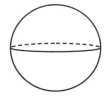   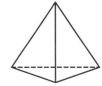   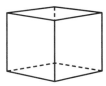

Solid: _____

Identifying Solid Figures Classifying Solids

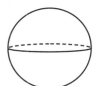   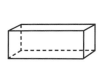   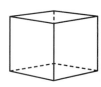

sphere   cone   triangular   cylinder   rectangular   cube
                    pyramid   prism

Look at each solid above. Then, complete the chart.

Name of Solid	Number of Faces	Shapes of Faces	Number of Vertices	Number of Edges
1.	1	circle	1	0
2.		square	8	12
3. rectangular prism		rectangle, square	8	
4.			4	
5. cylinder		circle	0	0
6.	0	no faces		0

Name _____ **Date** _____

  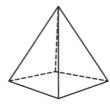 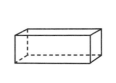

| sphere | cone | square pyramid | cylinder | rectangular prism | cube |

Write the name of the solid that matches each description.

1. I have six square faces.

_____

2. I have only one circular face.

_____

3. I have five faces and five vertices.

_____

4. I have no faces, edges, or vertices.

_____

5. I have at least four rectangular faces and 12 edges.

_____

6. I have two faces and one curved surface.

_____

Roll Four-in-a-Row

Materials: I die, two colors of crayons or pencils

To play: Players take turns. Player I rolls the die and checks the key to see what she can color. Color a space with that shape. If there are none left, you lose your turn. The first player to color four shapes in a row wins the game. The row can go up, down, across, or diagonally.

$\boxdot$ = cube $\vdots$ = triangular pyramid   = sphere

= cone   = rectangular prism   = cylinder

Round I

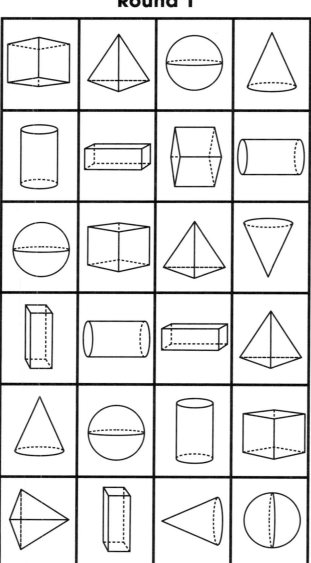

Round 2

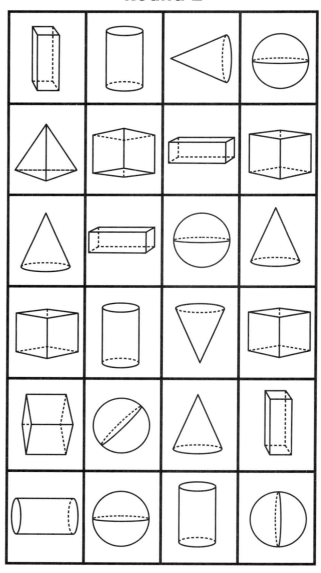

Partitioning Shapes

? Essential Question

How can a shape be partitioned into equal parts?

© Warm-Up/Review

Give a sheet of paper to each pair of students. Say, "You and your friend both want to draw but you only have one sheet of paper between you. What can you do so that each of you has an equal amount of paper to draw on?" Have students discuss how to divide the paper into equal shares.

★ Mini-Lesson

Materials: blank paper

1. Introduce and define the terms *partition*, *row*, and *column*.

2. Give students blank sheets of paper. Direct them to fold the papers in half horizontally and then open them again. Have them draw a line along the fold. Discuss how many equal parts the sheets of paper have been folded into.

3. Have students refold the sheets of paper in half as in step 1 and then fold them in half a second time. When students open their sheets of paper, they will see four equal parts. Have them draw a line along the new fold. Discuss how many rows and columns the rectangle has been folded into now. (2 rows, 2 columns)

4. Draw a square on the board and partition it into 9 equal parts. Explain that the square has been partitioned into 3 rows and 3 columns, creating 9 equal parts. Ask students where they may have seen something like this before. (Possible answers may include a tic-tac-toe board or a quilt.)

5. Continue providing examples of rectangles partitioned into equal parts. Then, have students draw and partition several rectangles.

💬 Math Talk

Why is it important to use equal units when partitioning a shape?
How do you know the partitions are equal?
Tell about an instance where you used partitioning in real life.

✏️ Journal Prompt

The cafeteria is serving lasagna for lunch. Each square pan of lasagna is cut into 4 rows and 4 columns. How many servings of lasagna are in each pan? Draw a picture to explain your thinking.

Materials

square tiles
graph paper

 Workstations

Activity sheets (pages 179–181)
Square Off! (page 182)

 Guided Math

⊙ **Remediation: Equal Parts**

1. Draw two rectangles to represent candy bars. Divide the first rectangle into four unequal parts. Divide the second rectangle into four equal parts. Ask students, "Which candy bar is divided evenly? How do you know?" Explain that the second rectangle is divided evenly because each section is the same size.

2. Distribute square tiles to students. Explain that each square is a square unit. Pose the following problem to students: *Shelby is planting a square garden. She wants to plant 9 different types of seeds, but she wants each seed type to be in its own equal section of the garden.* Have students model a square garden using the tiles.

3. Have students draw a map of the garden. Students should be able to explain why they divided the garden the way they did.

▢ **On Level: Partitioning with Arrays**

1. Distribute square tiles to students. Discuss how each tile is a square unit. Explain that you are working on making a rectangular quilt that is 4 square units wide by 5 square units long. Ask, "If the area is 4 squares wide and 5 squares long, how many squares will I need in all?" Allow time for students to explore with the tiles to develop an answer.

2. Model an array as a strategy to solve the problem. Say, "I need an area 5 square units long and 4 square units wide." Place 5 tiles going down. Place 3 more tiles going across beside the top tile. "Now, I must fill in the space." Fill the rectangular space with tiles. "To find the answer, I can count each tile individually. Or, I can use repeated addition: 5 + 5 + 5 + 5 or 4 + 4 + 4 + 4 + 4." Point to each column and then row as you say each.

3. Distribute graph paper to students. Pose the following problem: *Miguel wants to make a rectangular birthday cake that has 6 columns and 5 rows. Draw the cake.* Have students model their answers on the graph paper and write repeated addition sentences for the drawings.

4. Continue providing similar problems for students to solve.

▲ **Enrichment: Creating Partitioned Rectangles**

1. Give each student 18 tiles. Explain that each tile is a square unit. Ask students to create partitioned rectangles using these tiles. Explain that all of the tiles must be used, and each array should create a rectangle with no gaps or overlaps. No tiles can be hanging off of the edge.

2. Have students record their arrays on graph paper. Ask, "Can the same 18 tiles be arranged in a different way?" Challenge students to arrange the 18 tiles in all of the three possible ways. (1 x 18, 2 x 9, 3 x 6) Look for mistakes, such as adding an extra row. Have students record their arrays as repeated addition (6 square units + 6 square units + 6 square units = 18 square units).

3. Pose the following problem to students: *Maria lost her lunch money on the playground. To find it, her friends partitioned the playground into square units. Then, they each searched one square unit. If there were 6 square units in each row and 5 rows total, how many friends helped her search?* Students should model their answers on graph paper.

4. Have students create their own rectangular array word problems to solve with partners.

 Assess and Extend

Draw four rectangles on the board. Have students copy the rectangles and partition them equally in four different ways.

Partitioning Shapes

Look at each rectangle. Answer the questions.

1. Number of rows? _____

Number of columns? _____

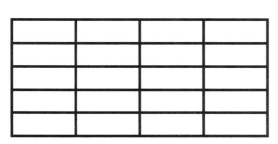

2. Number of rows? _____

Number of columns? _____

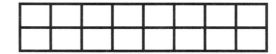

3. Number of rows? _____

Number of columns? _____

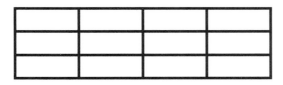

4. Partition this rectangle equally into 5 columns and 3 rows.

5. Partition this rectangle equally into 4 rows and 5 columns.

6. Partition this rectangle equally into 4 columns and 2 rows.

Partitioning Shapes ▪ Partitioning with Arrays

Use each grid to make the rectangle described.

1. 5 rows and 3 columns

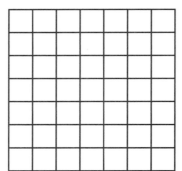

2. 1 row and 3 columns

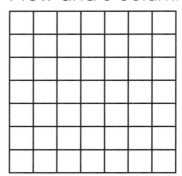

3. 4 rows and 4 columns

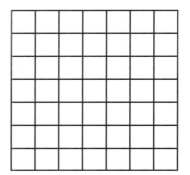

4. 5 rows and 2 columns

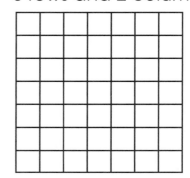

5. Partition this rectangle equally into 6 columns and 2 rows.

How many parts did you draw? _____

6. Partition this rectangle equally into 4 rows and 5 columns.

How many parts did you draw? _____

Partitioning Shapes ▲ Creating Partitioned Rectangles

Using color tiles or square pattern blocks, make and record as many different rectangles as you can with the given number.

1. 8 squares

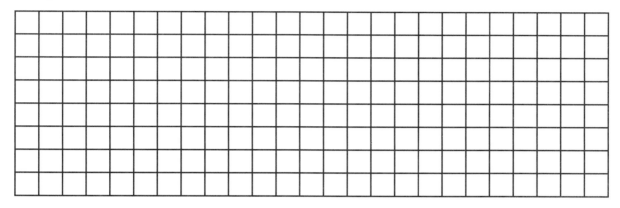

2. 10 squares

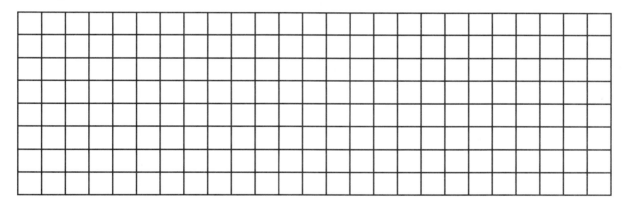

3. 12 squares

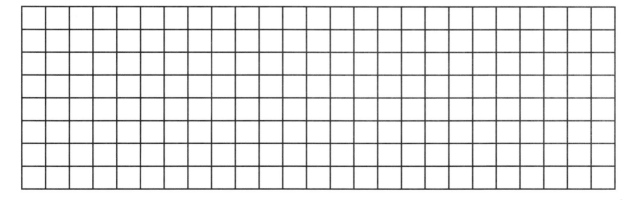

Square Off!

Materials: two colors of counters, 1 die, two colors of markers, calculator

To play: To begin play, each player places his counter on the Start space. Players take turns. Roll the die and move that many spaces. Follow the instructions to draw the rectangular partition on the grid. Inside the rectangle, write how many units make up the rectangle. Play until no more rectangles can be made, or until time is up. The player that creates non-overlapping rectangles with the most total square units wins.

Start →	3 rows by 1 column	2 rows by 5 columns	1 row by 3 columns	3 rows by 4 columns	5 rows by 4 columns	2 rows by 2 columns	4 rows by 2 columns	2 rows by 4 columns	1 row by 2 columns
1 row by 5 columns									4 rows by 4 columns
5 rows by 3 columns									3 rows by 2 columns
5 rows by 2 columns	3 rows by 5 columns	4 rows by 5 columns	1 row by 3 columns	4 rows by 3 columns	2 rows by 3 columns	4 rows by 1 column	5 rows by 1 column	1 row by 4 columns	3 rows by 3 columns

hundreds	tens	ones

Number of the Day

Word Form

Show it with base ten blocks.

Expanded Form

Place it on a number line.

$\longleftrightarrow$

This number is:
even   odd

Prove it.

Write the number that is

10 more	10 less
100 more	100 less

Ways to Make It

1._____
2._____
3._____
4._____
5._____

Use >, <, or = to compare it to yesterday's number of the day.

___ ◯ ___

Use it in a word problem.

_____
_____
_____
_____

Solve.

Count back.   **Count forward.**

←_____   _____→

____, ____, ____, [ ], ____, ____, ____,

Materials: 2 dice, 10 markers or counters (in two colors) per player

To play: Players take turns. Roll the dice and _____.
Cover the answer. You can "bump" the other player off of a space if there is only one counter on it. Once you place two counters on a space, it is yours and cannot be bumped. The player to use all of his or her counters first wins.

BUMP!

- ✂

To prep: Complete the title with the skill. Fill in the spaces with possible answers. Complete the directions with instructions related to the skill that describe how students use the numbers they roll. For example, *multiply the numbers* or *add, then cover the number that is two less.* Cut these directions off before copying. If desired, copy on cardstock and laminate for durability. Place it in a station with the related materials.

_____ Four-in-a-Row

Materials: _____ dice, two different colors of counters.

To play: Players take turns. _____
_____. Place your counter on the answer. If a counter is already on a space, you may not place a counter on the same space. The first player with four counters in a row wins.

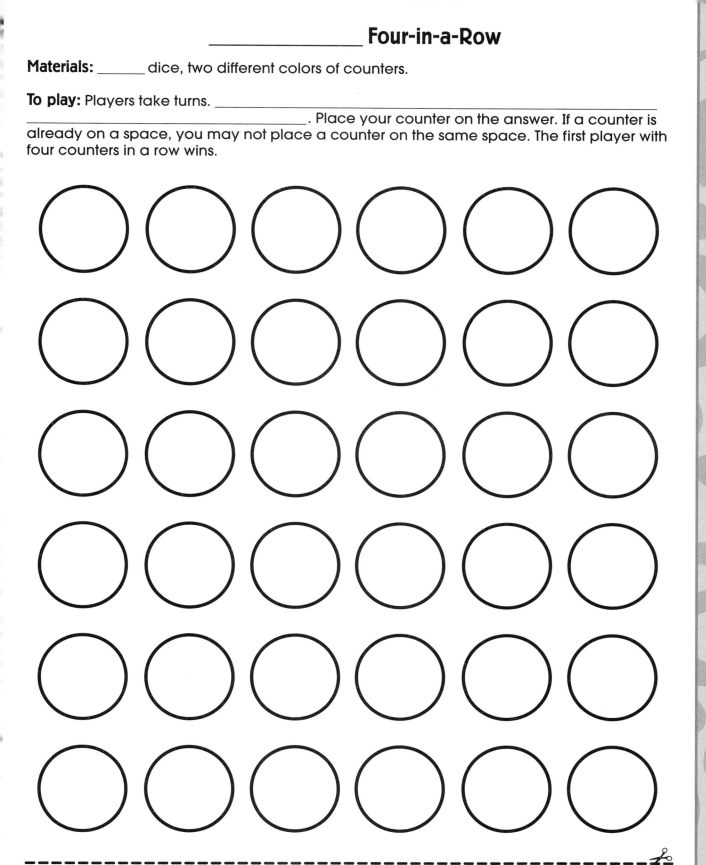

To prep: Fill in the circles with numbers. Place the numbers in random order and repeat numbers throughout. Fill in the number of dice needed in the Materials section. Complete the directions with instructions specific to the skill. For example, _roll two dice and add the numbers,_ or _roll three dice, place the numbers in any order to create a three-digit number, and round it to the nearest ten._ Cut off these directions before copying. If desired, copy it on cardstock and laminate for durability. Place it in a station with the related materials.

Path Game

Materials: I die, I counter or game piece for each player

To play: Players take turns. Roll the die. Move forward that many spaces. Solve the problem or follow the instructions on the space. If using cards, draw a card and solve the problem. If you answer correctly, stay on the space. If you answer incorrectly, return to your previous space. The first player to reach the Finish space wins.

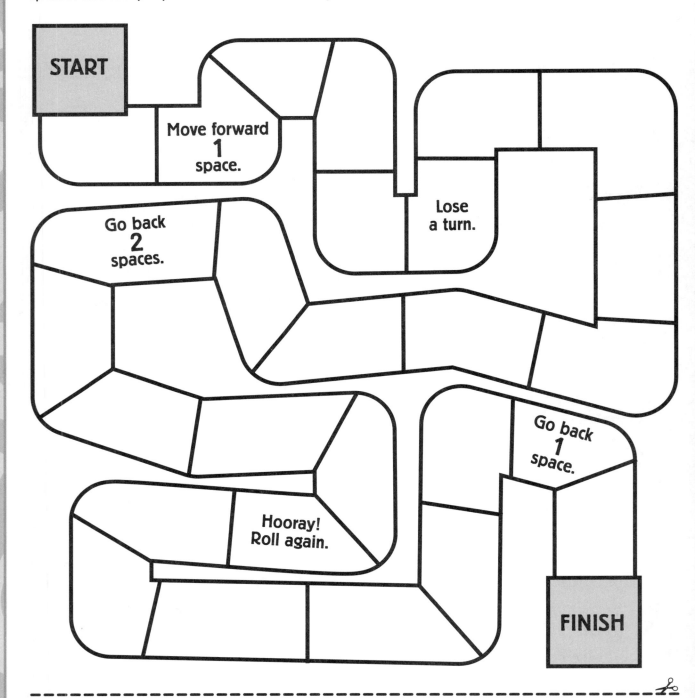

- ✂

To prep: Fill in the title with a fun or skill-based name. If using cards, add them to the materials list and create cards with problems or prompts on cardstock or index cards. If not using cards, write problems directly on the blank spaces. Cut off these directions before copying. If desired, copy them on cardstock and laminate for durability. Place them in a station with the related materials.

_____ Roll and Solve

Materials: I die

To play: Roll the die. Find the matching column and solve the bottom problem. Continue rolling and solving the next problem in each column until one column is complete. Color the winning animal. Continue to see which animals win second and third place.

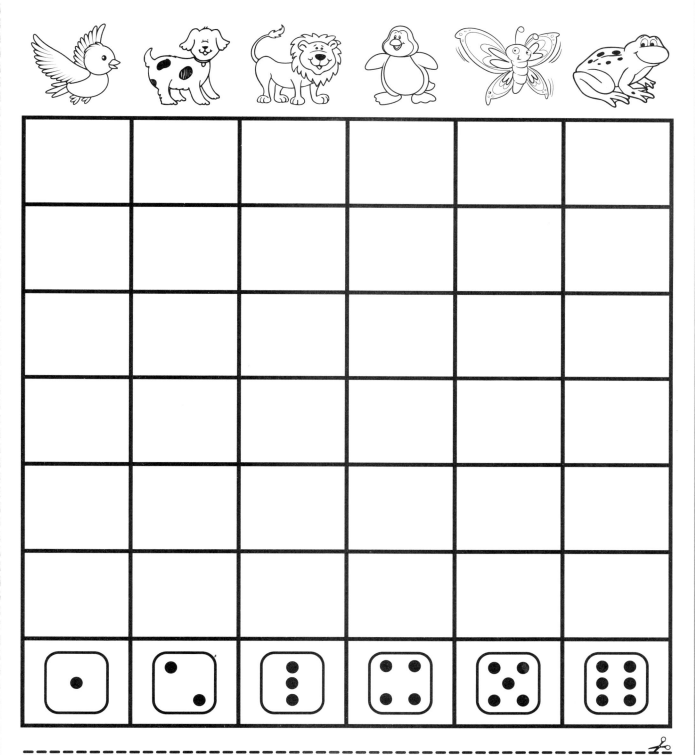

- ✂

To prep: Complete the title with the skill. Fill in the spaces below each animal with different problems. Cut off these directions before copying. If desired, copy them on cardstock and laminate for durability. Place them in a station with the related materials.

_____ Flip!

To play: Shuffle the cards. Place them all facedown. Players take turns. The first player flips over one card and _____. If the player answers correctly, he may keep the card. If not, return the card facedown to the pile. Once all of the cards have been flipped, the player with the most cards wins.

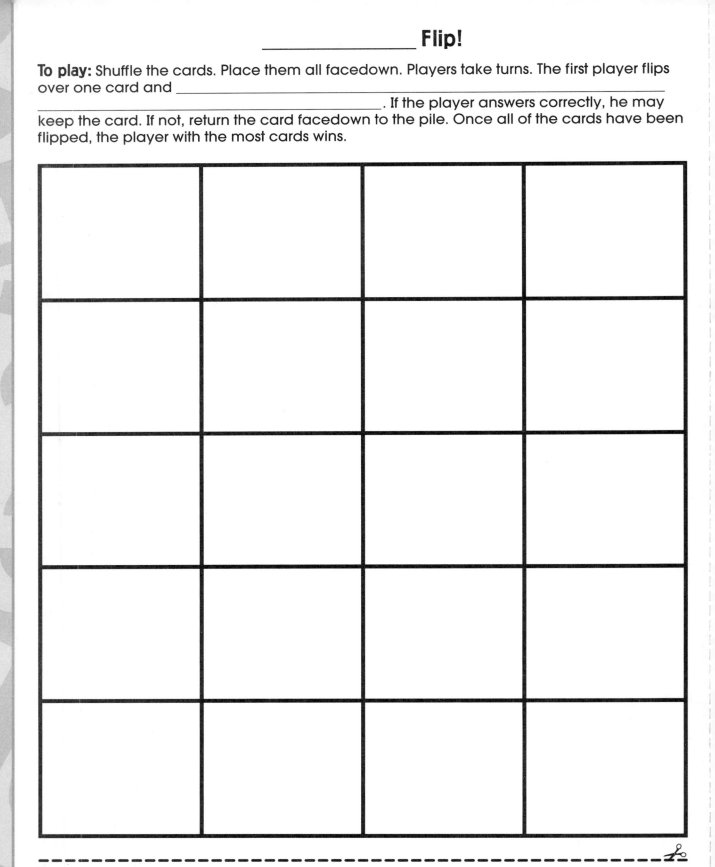

To prep: Complete the title with the skill. Fill in the cards with numbers or other prompts, such as geometric figures, angles, or shapes. Complete the directions by telling how students should answer or solve the prompts on the cards. For example, _tell what type of angle is shown_, or _tell how many to add to make 10_. Copy the cards on cardstock for durability and laminate if desired. Place them in a center with the directions. You may include a spatula and paper plates with the activity for students to use when "flipping" the cards and maintaining their "keep" piles.

_____ Shut the Box

Materials: _____ dice, _____ counters per person

To play: Cover all of the spaces on your board with counters. Players take turns. Roll the dice. _____
_____ If it has already been uncovered, mark one of your strikes. After one player has gotten three strikes, the player who has removed the most counters wins. Or, the first player to remove all of the counters without getting three strikes wins.

Player 1

Strike ① ② ③

Strike ① ② ③

Player 2

✂ -

To prep: Complete the title with the skill. Fill in the spaces on each section with the possible answers. Both sections should have the same numbers. You do not have to fill in all of the spaces. Complete the materials section with the number of dice and counters needed. Complete the directions with instructions related to the skill that describe how students use the numbers they roll. For example, *double the number, then uncover the answer,* or *add, then uncover the sum.* Cut off these directions before copying. If desired, copy them on cardstock and laminate for durability. Place them in a station with the related materials.

Answer Key

Page 17
1. C, 11; 2. E, 10; 3. F, 5; 4. A, 8;
5. D, 16; 6. B, 16

Page 18
1. 15 − 9 = 6; 2. 6 + 5 = 11;
3. 13 − 4 = 9; 4. 4 + 8 = 12;
5. 3 + 7 = 10; 6. 17 − 9 = 8 trading
cards; 7. 15 + 12 = 27 side salads;
8. 14 − 8 = 6 sunflowers

Page 19
Answers will vary but may
include: 1. 2 × 6 = 12, 6 + 6 = 12;
2. 3 × 9 = 27, 9 + 18 = 27;
3. 5 × 3 = 15, 10 + 5 = 15,
15 − 5 = 10; 4. 3 × 6 = 18,
12 + 6 = 18, 18 − 12 = 6;
5. 4 × 7 desks = 28;
6. 8 × 10 = 80 pounds

Page 23
Check students' work.
1. 9 − 4 = 5 flowers;
2. 12 + 5 = 17 pieces;
3. 12 − 6 = 6 more chickens;
4. 13 − 11 = 2 beads

Page 24
Check students' work. 1. 5 + ? =
16; 11; 2. 15 + ? = 26; 11; 3. 7 + ? =
22; 15; 4. 16 + ? = 24; 8; 5. ? + 13 =
30; 17; 6. 30 + ? = 55; 25

Page 25
Check students' work. Answers
will vary. 1. 12; 2. 40; 3. 12; 4. 59

Page 26
A. 8; B. 26; C. 21; D. 34; E. 15; F. 31;
G. 17; H. 17

Page 29
Check students' work.

Page 30
1. 50, 52, 54, 56; even; 2. 37, 39,
41, 43; odd; 3. 22, 24, 26, 28;
even; 4. 75, 77, 79, 81; odd; 5. 66,
68, 70, 72; even; 6. 11, 13, 15, 17;
odd; 7. 83, 85, 87, 89; odd; 8. 94,
96, 98, 100; even; 9. 19, 21, 23, 25,
27, 29; 10. 108, 106, 104, 102, 100,
98, 96; 11. 59, 57, 55, 53, 51; 12. 44,
46, 48, 50, 52, 54, 56

Page 31
1. 85, 84, yes; 2. 28, 27, no;
3. 51, 50, yes; 4. 98, 99, no;
5. 63, 64, yes; 6. 927, 926, yes;
7. 14 headlights; 8. 24 socks;
9. 38 shoes

Page 35
1. 18, 21, 24; 2. 21, 25, 29; 3. 7, 5,
3; 4. 20, 15, 10; 5. 18, 20, 22; 6. 32,
38, 44; 7. 13, 9, 5; 8. 31, 36, 41;
9. 13, 10, 7; 10. 15, 9, 3

Page 36
1. 31, +2; 2. 21, −3; 3. 31, +6; 4. 22,
−4; 5. 28, +5; 6. 74, +10; 7. 24, −8;
8. 46, −9; 9. 73, +12; 10. 41, −15;
11. 47, −7; 12. 132, +23

Page 37
1. 41, 57, 61; +4; 2. 26, 20, 12; −2;
3. 47, 65, 74; +9; 4. 46, 86, 96; +10;
5. 88, 79, 76; −3; 6. 50, 44, 38; −6;
7. 23, 55, 63; +8; 8. 32, 44, 58;
9. 27, 16, 4; 10. 125, 95, 60; 11. 64,
85, 109; 12. 38, 44, 51

Page 38
Check students' work.

Page 41
1. 8; 2. 20; 3. 1, 1, 1, 1, 1, 1, 1, 7;
4. 3, 3, 3, 3, 3, 15; 5. 4, 4, 4, 4, 16;
6. 3, 3, 3, 3, 12

Page 42
Accept all related multiplcation
sentenes. 1. 2 sets of 3; 2 × 3 = 6;
2. 4 sets of 2; 4 × 2 = 8; 3. 3 sets of
5; 3 × 5 = 15; 4. 2 sets of 4;
2 × 4 = 8; 5. 4 sets of 4;
4 × 4 = 16; 6. 1 set of 5; 1 × 5 = 5;
7. 5 sets of 4; 5 × 4 = 20; 8. 5 sets
of 2; 5 × 2 = 10

Page 43
Accept all related addition and
multiplcation sentenes.
1. 6 + 6 + 6 + 6 = 24; 4 × 6 = 24;
2. 9 + 9 = 18; 2 × 9 = 18;
3. 5 + 5 + 5 = 15; 3 × 5 = 15;
4. 7 + 7 = 14; 2 × 7 = 14;
5. 9 + 9 + 9 = 27; 3 × 9 = 27;
6. 3 + 3 + 3 + 3 = 12; 4 × 3 = 12;
7. 6 + 6 = 12; 2 × 6 = 12;
8. 8 + 8 + 8 = 24; 3 × 8 = 24

Page 47
1. 7, 3; 2. 1, 8; 3. 2, 4, 9; 4. 4, 0, 5;
5. 3, 1, 7; 6. 3 tens = 30; 7. 2 ones
= 2; 8. 7 tens = 70; 9. 6 hundreds
= 600; 10. 8 hundreds = 800

Page 48
1. 30 + 7 = 37; 2. 40 + 2 = 42;
3. 100 + 50 + 4 = 154; 4. 200 + 10
+ 8 = 218; 5. 500 + 3 = 503; 6. 300
+ 70 = 370; 7. 400 + 10 + 9; 8. 200
+ 80; 9. 700 + 30 + 5; 10. 600 + 7;
11. 935; 12. 408; 13. 312; 14. 860

Page 49
1. 341 = 300 + 40 + 1; 2. 1,208 =
1,000 + 200 + 8; 3. 450 = 400 + 50;
4. 506 = 500 + 6; 5. 760; 6. 3,016;
7. 2,080; 8. 901; 9. 1,312

Page 53
1. 252; 2. 528; 3. 285; 4. 603;
5. 539; 6. 420; 7. 191

Page 54
Check students' work. 1. 400 + 0
+ 2; 2. 500 + 20 + 3; 3. 600 + 30 +
0; 4. 200 + 40 + 1; 5. 0 + 80 + 7;
6. 400 + 70 + 2

Page 55
1. tens, 30; 2. ones, 7;
3. hundreds, 700; 4. hundreds,
600; 5. tens, 30; 6. hundreds, 400;
7. hundreds, 200; 8. tens, 40;
9. ones, 1; 10. thousands, 1,000;
11. 900 + 70 + 1; 12. 100 + 40 + 5;
13. 80 + 6; 14. 200 + 30; 15. 900 +
50 + 2

Page 59
1. 30; 2. 40; 3. 35; 4. 35, 50; 5. 60,
90, 100; 6. 60, 65, 70, 80; 7. 135,
155, 160, 165; 8. 10, 30, 50, 60, 80

Page 60
1. 455, 460, 465, 470; 2. 740, 745,
750, 755; 3. 265, 270, 275, 280;
4. 330, 335, 340, 345; 5. 120, 130,
140, 150; 6. 445, 455, 465, 475;
7. 950, 960, 970, 980; 8. 675, 685,
695, 705; 9. 130, 530, 630, 730;
10. 590, 690, 790, 890; 11. 595,
695, 795, 895; 12. 624, 724, 824,
924

Answer Key

Page 61
1. 2 × 5 = 10; 2. 3 × 5 = 15;
3. 6 × 5 = 30; 4. 5 × 5 = 25;
5. 30 seeds; 6. 50 slices

Page 65
1. 29, 31; 31; 2. 54, 53; 54; 3. 60,
70; 70; 4. 30, 24; 30; 5. 115, 223;
223; 6. 68, 50; 7. 21, 27; 8. 34, 43

Page 66
1. 64; 65; 2. 218; 223; 3. 430; 435;
4. >; 5. <; 6. >; 7. >; 8. <; 9. >;
10–12. Check students' work.

Page 67
1. 58, 85, 95; 2. 25, 32, 53; 3. 147,
157, 174; 4. 304, 340, 430; 5. 509,
590, 591; 6. 76, 716, 761; 7. 49, 483,
487; 8. <; 9. >; 10. =; 11. <; 12. >;
13. <; 14. >, >; 15. >, =

Page 71
1. 17; 2. 27; 3. 32; 4. 19; 5. 18; 6. 21;
7. 20; 8. 17; 9. 22; 10. 22

Page 72
Check students' work. Answers
will vary.

Page 73
Check students' work. 1. 46;
2. 51; 3. 62; 4. 90; 5. 82; 6. 60

Page 77
1. 79; 2. 88; 3. 55; 4. 52; 5. 95;
6. 90; 7. 58; 8. 83; 9. 121; 10. 165

Page 78
1. 90; 2. 81; 3. 73; 4. 60; 5. 82;
6. 70; 7. 75; 8. 77; 9. 57; 10. 83;
11. 74; 12. 80; 13. 95; 14. 101;
15. 90; 16. 85; 17. 47; 18. 81; 19. 67;
20. 40

Page 79
1. 561; 2. 811; 3. 953; 4. 740; 5. 242;
6. 700; 7. 815; 8. 568; 9. 820;
10. 832; 11. 912; 12. 611; 13. 687; 14.
1,020; 15. 610; 16. 921; 17. 824; 18.
673; 19. 532; 20. 541

Page 83
1. 72; 2. 73; 3. 82; 4. 71; 5. 87; 6. 92

Page 84
Check students' work. 1. 74;
2. 88; 3. 113; 4. 153; 5. 120; 6. 119

Page 85
1. 381; 2. 1,535; 3. 2,080; 4. 936;
5. 793; 6. 2,794; 7. 704; 8. 3,230;
9. 794

Page 89
1. 7; 2. 9; 3. 9; 4. 5; 5. 8; 6. 9; 7. 7;
8. 9; 9. 8; 10. 5; 11. 6; 12. 2; 13. 8;
14. 1; 15. 15; 16. 30; 17. 32; 18. 27;
19. 38; 20. 33; 21. 31; 22. 33; 23. 34;
24. 31; 25. 30

Page 90
1. 81; 2. 52; 3. 179; 4. 64; 5. 448;
6. 73; 7. 90; 8. 85; 9. 287; 10. 976;
11. 300; 12. 141

Page 91
1. 231; 2. 115; 3. 134; 4. 233; 5. 544;
6. 100; 7. 743; 8. 102

Page 95
1. 34 – 16 = 18; 2. 61 – 29 = 32;
3. 28; 4. 14; 5. 27; 6. 39; 7. 23; 8. 16

Page 96
1. 46; 2. 36; 3. 58; 4. 7; 5. 11; 6. 19;
7. 28; 8. 77; 9. 19; 10. 48; 11. 16;
12. 69; 13. 47; 14. 26; 15. 19; 16. 8;
17. 5; 18. 27; 19. 29; 20. 81

Page 97
Check students' work. 1. 12;
2. 68; 3. 29; 4. 45; 5. 24; 6. 377;
7. 376; 8. 532

Page 101
Check students' work. 1. 41;
2. 143; 3. 220; 4. 377; 5. 532; 6. 199

Page 102
1. 106, 306; 2. 665, 865; 3. 313,
513; 4. 788, 988; 5. 207, 407;
6. 744, 944; 7. 30, 230; 8. 271, 471;
9. 562, 762; 10. 122, 322; 11. 340,
540; 12. 528, 728; 13. 230, 430;
14. 164, 364; 15. 190, 390; 16. 449,
649; 17. 531, 731; 18. 770, 970;
19. 708, 908; 20. 800, 1,000

Page 103
1. 156 pages; 2. 288 books;
3. 173 minutes; 4. 100 pages;
5. 200 more words; 6. 325 books

Page 107
1. tape measure; 2. ruler; 3. tape
measure; 4. meterstick; 5. ruler;
6. meterstick; 7. yardstick; 8. ruler

Page 108
1. 3 cm; 2. 6 ft.; 3. 20 in.; 4. 1 yd.;
5. 5 ft.; 6. 10 in.; 7. 7 cm;
8. 100 yd.; 9. 6 in.; 10. 15 m

Page 109
Explanations will vary. 1. 5-foot
ladder; 2. no; 3. tape measure;
4. yes

Page 113
1. 2 in., 5 cm; 2. 1 in., 3 cm;
3. 5 in., 13 cm; 4. 4 in., 10 cm;
5. 2 in., 5 cm; 6. 3 in., 8 cm;
7. 2 in., 5 cm; 8. 5 in., 13 cm

Page 114
1. 2 in.; 2. 4 cm; 3. 4 in.; 4. 3 in.;
5. 2 cm; 6. 3 cm

Page 115
1–8. Check students' work.
9. twice; 10. 0 times

Page 119
Estimates will vary. 1. 1 in.
2. 2 cm; 3. 5 in. 4. 5 cm; 5. 6 in.
6. 4 in. 7. 7 cm; 8. 9 cm

Page 120
Estimates will vary. 1. 5 in.
2. 9 cm; 3. 2 in.; 4. 10 cm;
5. 2 cm; 6. 3 in.; 7. 17 cm;
8–10. Check students' work.

Page 121
1. Estimates will vary. A. 1 in.; B. 2
cm; C. 2 in.; D. 6 in.; E. 6 cm; 2–5.
Check students' work.

Page 125
1. 11 ft.; 2. 9 m; 3. 20 yd.; 4. 3 cm;
5. 18 ft.

Answer Key

Page 126
Check students' work. 1. 19 ft.;
2. 21 yd.; 3. 28 cm; 4. 16 ft.;
5. 45 m

Page 127
1. 17 in;. 2. 15 m; 3. 9 yd.;
4–5. Check students' work.

Page 131
1. A; 2. C; 3. E; 4. F; 5. D; 6. B

Page 132
1. 5:30; 2. 7:10; 3. 3:45; 4. 9:20;
5. 11:55; 6. 4:15; 7. 2:35; 8. 6:05;
9. 8:30; 10. seven forty-five or
quarter till eight; 11. ten thirty or
half past ten; 12. twelve fifteen
or quarter past twelve

Page 133
1. 5; 2. 3:40; 3. 9:20; 4. 3; 5. 4; 6. 2

Page 137
1. 1, 2, 3, 4, 5, 6, 7, 8, 8¢; 2. 25, 50,
75, 100, 100¢ or $1.00; 3. 10, 20,
30, 40, 50, 60, 70, 70¢; 4. 5, 10, 15,
20, 25, 30, 30¢; 5. 5, 10, 15, 20, 25,
30, 35, 40, 40¢; 6. 25, 50, 75, 100,
125, 125¢ or $1.25

Page 138
Answers will vary.

Page 139
Check students' work. 1. $1.90;
2. $0.75; 3. $0.58; 4. $5.35;
5. $3.50; 6. $6; 7. $5.20; 8. $3.80

Page 143
Check students' work. apple = 7;
banana = 6; pear = 4;
pineapple = 3; basketball = 2;
baseball = 4; football = 6;
soccer = 8

Page 144
Check students' work.
1. small = 8; medium = 5;
large = 11; 11 T-shirts; 2. won = 18;
lost = 8; tied = 2; won;
3. bus = 24; car = 6; walk = 6;
24 students

Page 145
Check students' work.

Page 149
1. 5 sunflowers; 2. 2 sunflowers;
3. 7 ft.; 4. 12 ft.; 5. Check
students' work.

Page 150
Check students' work.
1. 1 necklace; 2. 2 necklaces;
3. Check students' work.
4. 11 necklaces

Page 151
Check students' work. 1. 4 cm,
6 cm; 2. 6 bean sprouts;
3. 24 bean sprouts; 4. 3 bean
sprouts

Page 155
1. 1 basket made; 2. Trisha;
3. 5 baskets; 4. Caden;
5. 7 baskets; 6. 3 baskets

Page 156
1. Ashley; 2. 10 seeds; 3. Jeremy;
4. Zach; 5. 4 seeds; 6. 18 seeds;
7. 8 seeds; 8. 36 seeds

Page 157
1. mystery; 2. 4 biographies;
3. 6 more; 4. sports; 5. 5 more;
6. 29 books; 7. Each amount
would be half of what it is.

Page 161
Check students' work.
1. 7 customers; 2. brownie;
3. ice cream; 4. 4 more;
5. 13 customers; 6. 23 customers

Page 162
1. giraffe; 2. 7 students; 3. The
number of students is equal to
the number in between. 4. The
bar for the tiger is taller than the
bar for the panda, so the tiger
was more popular. 5. 4 more;
6. 13 students

Page 163
1. vanilla; 2. 9 customers; 3. 10
customers; 4. 4 customers; 5. 15
customers; 6. The bars for butter
pecan are the shortest on both
days, so it was the least favorite.
7. 21 customers; 8. 5 more

Page 164
A. Fast Learner; B. Great Helper
and Fast Learner; C. 2 more;
D. 22 awards; E. Fast Learner
and Well Behaved; F. Good
Listener; G. 12 awards; H. Good
Listener; I. 5 more

Page 167
Check students' work.

Page 168
1. A, B, E, F, I; 2. D; 3. G; 4. D, H;
5. A, B, C, D, E, F, H, I; 6. H; 7. A, B,
D, E, F, H, I; 8. A, I; 9. C, G; 10. A,
B, C, D, E, F, G, H, I

Page 169
1–6. Check students'
compositions. 1. triangle;
2. square; 3. hexagon;
4. rhombus; 5. rectangle;
6. square

Page 173
1. cylinder; 2. sphere;
3. rectangular prism;
4. triangular pyramid

Page 174
1. cone; 2. cube, 6; 3. 6, 12;
4. triangular pyramid, 4, triangle,
6; 5. 2; 6. sphere, 0

Page 175
1. cube; 2. cone; 3. square
pyramid; 4. sphere;
5. rectangular prism; 6. cylinder

Page 179
1. 5, 4; 2. 2, 8; 3. 3, 4; 4–6. Check
students' work.

Page 180
1–4. Check students' work. 5. 12;
6. 20

Page 181
Check students' work.